Comments from people who have read
TEA: The Recipe for Stress-Free Living

"A remarkable book that I couldn't put down.
It should be read again and again."

- Elizabeth H. Roybal
Realtor, wife and mother of two

"Awesome book! A must for all who have ever read
any related materials from other authors. I fully
endorse this book as a student of Truth."

- John Van Deilen
President, *Van Deilen Industries*

"It's just delightful, with an air of a light-hearted
whispiness and joy about it — a real treasure. I want
to be just like Swamiji when I grow up!"

- Wilhelmina "Billie" Kamis
President, *Willoughby Hills City Council*

"In a very simple dialogue, "TEA" provides a life-
changing recipe that frees us from the pains
associated with worldly living and gives us the
power to understand our purpose in this world!"

- Dr. A. Raj Chowdhury
Professor & Dean, *Kent State University*

TEA™

Dear Anju & Ajay,

This book is dedicated to to you with my utmost love and regards

Ratanjit

12/2/05

The Recipe for Stress-Free Living

Ratanjit
RATANJIT S. SONDHE

discoverhelp
publishing

Cleveland, Ohio

discoverhelp publishing, inc.
33095 Bainbridge Road, Cleveland, Ohio 44139, USA
www.discoverhelp.com

a discoverhelp, inc. company

discoverhelp publishing books may be purchased for educational or
business use. Special discounts may apply. For ordering information,
please contact the publisher: business@discoverhelp.com

TEA™ is a trademark of discoverhelp publishing, inc.

Printed in the United States of America.
First Edition

Library of Congress Control Number: 2005925725

ISBN-13: 978-1-59076-021-5
ISBN-10: 1-59076-021-2

Acknowledgement

To whom should I show gratitude?
Whose help I must proclaim?
How can I not express my thanks
To everyone by name?

In fact, the name upon this book
Is mine, but need not be.
For not a thought or word here writ
Did come from within me.

I am but a conduit
As electric power flows.
Each thought has come from somewhere else
And somewhere else it goes.

It matters not the "from" or "to,"
But what comes in between.
As light illumines darkened space
So hidden jewels are seen.

Yes, everyone along this line
Of power - No, of love,
Is most deserved for me to thank
And voice their role thereof.

But in such words of gracious praise
A tragedy is done.
For this has come from all of us.
And this is all from One.

Note from the Author:

This book came through me, but was not created by me. Its design and package were conceived by others around me. The heart and soul of this book was realized in a matter of minutes and written in but a week. However, putting it into a final, easy to read version was another story.

Each time I read this book, it brings a tear to my eye. Every reading is like my first and there is something new and intriguing that affects me in a different and special way. I find—as I hope you do—that it helps me to align my thoughts and guide my life without negativity, unfulfilled expectations and self-doubt. It has gifted me a life free of stress and frustration.

I hope that you will find this book, *TEA*, to have the same life-changing impact as it has had on me. I look forward to hearing from you.

Ratanjit
email@ratanjit.com

Contents of

TEA: The Recipe for Stress-Free Living

"A question always originates in the mind, whereas the true answer always lies in the heart."

Chapter One

STRESS AND FRUSTRATION

A s with all tales worthy of telling, ours begins gently with love...

David DeFario was born and raised in Southern California. From his earliest days in school, he found himself deeply interested in ancient literature and greatly intrigued by old-world wisdom. Even after completing his undergraduate degree, David still hungered to understand life's mysteries and his own purpose in life. He began searching for the right school and chose a well-known university on the other coast of America to study philosophy. It was there that he met Anju, the woman who would become his wife, as she worked toward her degree in clinical psychology.

Anju was born in India, and she had persuaded her

parents to allow her to complete her education in the United States. Anju's parents had been reluctant about allowing her to do so, fearing that the lovely ways of their daughter would steal the heart of a young American boy, and she would end up living far away from home. They were right.

David had always been fascinated with India and its mystical ways. Somehow, all of that was reflected in Anju, and he fell more in love with her every minute they were together. Anju fell in love with David's passion to make a difference and his inner quest for truth.

Towards the end of their Ph.D. studies, David asked Anju for her hand in marriage. Anju and David were excited to be part of each other's lives, but they wanted the blessing of both their parents before embarking on this new journey together.

When Anju's parents first learned of their daughter's desire to marry a person outside their caste and religion, they were disturbed and hesitant. It was only upon meeting David that they became deeply touched by his unselfish and loving ways and welcomed him with open arms into their family.

While David stayed with Anju's family for several days in India, they introduced him to a family friend, a monk from Katmandu, who was traveling through New Delhi and had become their houseguest for a day. In the brief time David spent with the monk, whom everyone referred to as Swamiji in a very respectful and loving way, David felt the depth and clarity of his wisdom and longed to spend more time with him. As David had come to learn through ancient Sanskrit, 'Swamiji' was an honored title given to one who had 'ownership of oneself' and was considered to be a divine master, teacher and guiding light in this world.

Upon returning to America, David brought Anju home to meet his parents in San Diego. David's mother, Patty, a retired psychologist, found Anju to be the daughter she never had.

David's father, Matthew, was counting the days to his retirement from the local phone company and eagerly awaited David's return home. He told his wife that he was a bit uncomfortable with David's decision not to marry an American girl, but that uneasiness quickly left as he saw how happy David and Anju were together.

Talking to one of her former colleagues, Patty learned that there was a new job opening at the hospital. Anju interviewed with flying colors and found herself having a job without even trying.

Not too long after, David became an associate professor at the University of California, San Diego.

David and Anju had a simple wedding ceremony and found themselves settled into the daily routine of their lives. Time passed quickly, and just after celebrating their second anniversary, Anju and David received a call from Swamiji informing them that he would be coming to the United States and would be able to spend some time with them.

Anju and David were overjoyed. They had often mentioned Swamiji in conversation to their dearest and closest friends and how his simple words of wisdom guided them to cope with life's unexpected challenges. From the first time David met Swamiji in New Delhi, he still remembered their time together. David felt the weight of Swamiji's presence and the peaceful glow on his face.

When the day for Swamiji's visit finally arrived, a total of ten people were invited including the host couple. There were Manmohan Singh, whom everyone called 'Manny,' and his wife, Mona. Manny was an up-and-coming businessman and Mona was an anesthesiologist. Anju and Mona crossed paths at the hospital and soon discovered they were both from New Delhi and spoke the same language. They shared many common interests such as Indian cooking, clothing and jewelry, but nothing surpassed their mutual love for Indian movies. For their part, Manny and David became good friends due to their passion for American football, politics and spicy foods.

Manny and Mona were born in India. Although their marriage was arranged, they were seemingly made for each other and had recently celebrated their fifth year as husband and wife.

David and Anju had also invited Ron and Susie Smith to this gathering. Ron was known for being extremely curious about everything. This curiosity inspired him to pursue a career studying the human brain, and he became a highly sought-after neurosurgeon. His lively and youthful-looking wife, Susie, was a successful realtor. Her outgoing personality made Susie very prominent in her field.

Ron and Mona worked together as a surgical team at the same hospital. Ron thought Mona was one of the most brilliant anesthesiologists he had ever worked with and would never perform a surgery without her in his OR. Initially, it was Mona who introduced Anju to Ron at the hospital. When Ron learned that Anju was becoming frustrated in search for her dream house, he introduced Susie to help her find the ideal place.

Susie had never met a woman as meek and likable as Anju, yet as demanding and strong-willed in her ways. Although very different in style and personality, Anju and Susie worked well together. During the search for Anju's perfect house, they discovered they had many common interests and soon became close friends.

Anju invited Marcie and Tony Chen. Marcie was an immigration attorney well known for handling the most difficult cases. She was also known for being outspoken about the legal system and the injustices she felt so many people chose to ignore. Marcie met Anju when helping with her immigration papers. Marcie also turned her on to the local art scene and it became a regular Saturday ritual for them to visit galleries, shows and events together.

Marcie's husband, Tony, was a man of few words, but he had a fire within him to become very successful. He was a Chinese immigrant whose family had experienced political scrutiny in his homeland. Wanting to make a new life for himself, Tony came to America. Only seven years later, he owned one of California's most successful consulting engineering firms.

David's mother, Patty, asked to attend the reception for Swamiji and offered to make her famous homemade cookies and serve tea. David had told her about his initial meeting with Swamiji in India, and she was anxious to hear him for herself.

Everyone was coming in at different times. Patty arrived early and was impatient to meet their honored guest. She asked Anju when he was scheduled to arrive. Before Anju could say anything, Marcie and Tony arrived. Marcie was sharing her frustration with Tony about the trial still on her mind from the night before. She simply could not comprehend how the judge completely disregarded the truth and ignored the arguments in her case.

Soon Mona walked in looking a bit upset because Manny was going to be late. His company was having a problem with one of its new products and he had to call an emergency Saturday morning meeting to try to get control of the situation. He told her that he would come directly from his office as soon as he could.

Just then, David arrived with Swamiji. A beautiful calmness filled the room and everyone became silent. Anju warmly welcomed Swamiji and introduced him to the guests who had already arrived. Swamiji greeted each person individually. It was obvious that he was deeply interested to learn about each of his guests.

As everyone waited for the final few to arrive,

refreshments were served. Anju was feeling stressed. She had wanted the afternoon to go perfectly, and they were already 20 minutes past their start time.

A few minutes later, Susie and Ron walked in. Ron was talking on his cell phone. Obviously upset and embarrassed, Susie said, "Anju, I'm sorry that we're so late, but it's your friend Ron who's to blame. He was late picking up the babysitter and he's been on that phone all day!"

Then Manny rushed in. He was grumbling, still thinking about the problems at the office. Mona immediately asked him, "Did you bring the fruit basket, Manny?"

Manny threw up his arms and immediately apologized. "I'm so sorry, I completely forgot to pick it up. I'll go back and get it."

Mona shook her head in disgust.

Anju felt for Manny and told him, "Don't worry, Manny. We have plenty of food. Come sit down and have a cup of tea."

David joked with his buddy, "I thought you started your own company to get away from working Saturdays." Manny shrugged and said, "I thought so, too."

Anju asked everyone to sit down and make themselves comfortable. Tea was served, and a tray filled with homemade goodies was passed around the room.

All were curiously waiting for the afternoon to unfold.

Patty poured Swamiji a cup of tea and gladly offered him both milk and honey, as he preferred. Her actions brought a thoughtful smile to his face. After taking a sip of the hot tea, he closed his eyes and took a deep breath. Suddenly, everyone was visibly drawn into Swamiji's calmness.

He opened his eyes and said, "Tea…ah…tea…um…" He smiled and continued slowly, in a soft tone, "In my travels around the world, seeing many families, business people, professionals, housewives, students, rich and poor, young and old, one thing that everyone experiences and faces is frustration."

"We *all* do," acknowledged Patty. "No one is free of frustration." The others nodded in agreement.

"Frustration results from our inability to change or control the situation. It happens when our expectations are not met, or we disagree with an action or decision made by someone else," Swamiji explained.

"What frustrates me the most is when people don't take responsibility for their own actions, and I have to pay the price," Marcie said quickly.

"It seems like I'm always at the mercy of others. Why don't people just do what they say they'll do?" asked Susie. "It frustrates the dickens out of me."

Pretty soon everyone was giving their own variation of why they were frustrated.

Swamiji remained quiet until David asked, "But there's always a reason for our frustration, isn't there?"

Swamiji replied, "Yes, there is always a reason or explanation, or even a blame that may fully justify our frustrations. It is these frustrations that cause us enormous havoc and outright debilitate us."

Ron agreed and shared his firsthand medical experience. "Frustration certainly is the seed for most of our stress, Swamiji. And stress is the root cause of high blood pressure, depression and obesity that lead to so many nasty diseases."

Patty had her own experiences as a psychologist and asked, "Sir, is there really a way to eliminate frustration from our life? How can we take back control of our lives and be free of frustration and stress?"

Marcie joined in. "How can it be possible to eliminate stress and frustration when we have so many responsibilities?"

Swamiji took a sip of his tea and said, "Actually it is so simple that most of us miss it."

In his heart, David felt he knew what Swamiji was saying, but his mind did not comprehend the words. "Swamiji, if it's so simple," he asked, "why can't we find the answer? What is it that we're missing?"

With a kind-hearted voice, Swamiji replied, "David, when we see from our mind's eyes, we are not able to unveil the total truth. Our mind is like a supercomputer that stores and computes the data and experiences it collects. Our mind then calculates an answer and either accepts or rejects it based upon past data and experiences. However, in its purest state and form, our heart taps directly into life's uncontaminated universal wisdom."

In a short breath, Swamiji continued, "My friends, a question always originates in the mind, whereas the true answer always lies in the heart."

There was a moment of silence until Manny posed a light-hearted question. "Swamiji, isn't there a 'simple' way for busy people like us to cope with our stress and frustration? Can't you suggest some sort of tea made from 'mountain-grown herbs'? Something that can make all of our stress and frustrations go away?"

Everyone who knew Manny smiled. He had a habit of kidding about everything.

Swamiji returned the smile, saying, "You could be right, Manny. Perhaps that is all we need to do... have a cup of tea and all our frustrations will go away."

Everyone laughed except Anju, who remained deep in thought. She wished it really was that simple to get rid of her stress and frustrations.

"In reality, it could be that simple," Swamiji said softly as if he had heard Anju's wish. "You really can get rid of all your frustration through a simple cup of *tea*...provided that you know the right *recipe* of this special tea."

Everyone was surprised at Swamiji's response. They were not sure if he was joking or serious.

Manny exclaimed, "Are you serious? There really *is* a *recipe*?"

Manny's business mind immediately began thinking. Was this recipe available? Could he patent it and sell it to the world? What would he call it? He turned over his napkin and began making notes. He was ready to write down this million-dollar recipe.

Somehow, David had a feeling that Swamiji was serious, yet he also knew that the recipe of this tea could not possibly consist of any worldly ingredients.

Swamiji had everyone's total attention, their silence an invitation for further explanation.

"To avoid stress and frustration, all we need to do is *have a cup of tea*," Swamiji repeated. "The recipe of this TEA, my friends, is hidden in each letter of the word *tea*...T-E-A."

Again, it was not the answer anyone expected.

"May I offer you the exclusive recipe of this TEA?" Swamiji asked.

Everyone nodded. They had no idea where Swamiji was heading, but wherever it was, they knew they wanted to follow.

"It is our heart,
not our mind,
that taps directly into
life's uncontaminated
universal wisdom."

Chapter Two

Wisdom of the Letter 'T'

"Each letter of the word TEA is full of incredible wisdom," began Swamiji. "Once we understand what each letter stands for, we will be empowered with all the wisdom that we will ever need to handle stress and frustration, regardless of its origin and intensity.

"The first letter of the word TEA is T, which stands for truth. But I speak of the real truth, not the perceived truth," said Swamiji. "In other words, our perception of reality is skewed and erroneous."

Swamiji tried to simplify further, "We do not see things as they really are, but from the reference point of our database of experiences. All of our beliefs and knowledge are relative truths because they are based on some arbitrary truth that we have learned or been taught. You see, even our perception of our personal life and its realities is incorrect.

"I'm not quite sure I follow, Swamiji," said Patty.

"You see, Patty," Swamiji replied, "the perceived truth, or information, that comes into us gets tainted by our fear, greed, insecurities, agendas and our ego. Even our understanding of who we are is misunderstood. Thus, all our realities and our truths are erroneous."

"But how can we *not* have a history of experiences and *not* maintain a database?" Ron asked. "Shouldn't these experiences be my realities?"

Swamiji took a deep breath and closed his eyes. There was pin-drop silence in anticipation of Swamiji's response. He opened his eyes and said, "If you took the most elegant, expensive and sweetest perfume and poured it into a bottle which had had garlic in it, would you be able to enjoy the fragrance of this beautiful perfume without the dominating odor of garlic?"

Swamiji continued, "Similarly, we are not able to experience the truth that is unadulterated, pure and unchangeable. All we see and talk about is a 'conditional truth' that has been tainted by our 'garlic' and never the real or absolute truth, which is undisputed, universal and timeless."

"The information
that comes into us
gets tainted by our
fear, greed, insecurities,
agendas and our ego."

"But we can see and feel the truth if we are honest with ourselves, can't we, Swamiji?" asked Anju.

Swamiji felt the hunger in Anju's tone for clarity and responded.

> Imagine for a moment a young, well-dressed woman who was just promoted to CEO of a major corporation walks into the corner coffee shop where four individuals wait to order their drinks. One is a New York fashion designer and another a health nutritionist and fitness coach. The third is a Fortune 500 senior executive and the fourth, a state legislator. Each of these four individuals has already formed an opinion about this woman through the tainted vision of their database without knowing a single real truth about her. The fashion designer judges her by the clothes she wears. The health and fitness coach is impressed by her physique. The senior executive would never think she is a CEO without seeing her business card, and the state legislator immediately labels her a Republican based on her conservative business attire.

"Isn't that what we do every day?" asked Swamiji.

Nodding thoughtfully, Manny posed a question. "Doesn't science tell us the real truth?"

Swamiji decided to answer this question with another example. "Manny, you told me that you are constructing a new building for your business. Let's suppose that you used the most brilliant architect and the most competent builders, but there was an error in the architect's computer program. Every place that it should have calculated a 'one,' it calculated everything as a 'two.' Your building would not meet your expectations and could even collapse," said Swamiji. "Despite the efforts of all of these most qualified professionals, your facts and truths were erroneous, because your architect was using a faulty computer program. Everyone would be completely frustrated. They were sure they had done everything correctly and still, they did not understand the reason for their failure."

After a brief pause, Swamiji continued, "Our perception of life itself is incorrect. Even our understanding of *who we are* is flawed. Hence, all of our realities and truths are erroneous."

Parts of what Swamiji said rang true in their hearts, yet he felt they were not able to fully understand all that he said.

"Even our understanding
of who we are is flawed.
Hence, all of our realities
and truths are erroneous."

Swamiji gently smiled and said, "Let me share an old-time story with you..."

Immediately, a child-like smile appeared on Anju's face. From the time she was a little girl, she always adored and was fascinated by Swamiji's stories.

Swamiji settled back in his chair and with ocean-like depth in his eyes began.

Once upon a time, there was a wonderful kingdom with a highly spiritual king by the name of Maharaja Shamsher Singh. The king had a son who he named Mehar Singh. He chose 'Mehar' because the word meant 'God's blessing.'

The king raised his son under the supervision and training of highly learned and spiritual gurus. He also had an assistant and bodyguard named Murli to aid and watch over him.

Prince Mehar grew up in a kingdom filled with mountains, forests and rivers. He loved to experience the vast wonders of the kingdom for weeks at a time, exploring new horizons of untouched nature. The Prince and Murli would often get lost in the wilderness, but Prince Mehar's uncanny sense of direction would always lead them back on the right path.

One day, Prince Mehar was traveling with Murli on horseback through the jungle. They encountered some very rough terrain, and when his horse lost his footing, the Prince slipped off his horse and landed hard on his foot cutting his toe. Being far from the kingdom, it took several days for the Prince to receive medical attention, and by that time, his little toe was terribly infected and could not be saved.

"I'm sure he was very upset," said David's mother, Patty, feeling sorry for the Prince.

"Actually," Swamiji responded, "Prince Mehar accepted the situation without concern, but Murli was deeply troubled."

When Murli saw the Prince and learned what had happened, Murli cried, "God, this is such a wonderful and handsome Prince. Why did you have to disfigure him?" Murli could not understand why God would allow this to happen to such an honorable and kind person.

The Prince consoled his loyal assistant and told him, "Have faith in the wisdom of the universe, my friend. There is always a reason why things happen."

"It does seem that bad things always happen to good people," Mona interrupted.

"It may seem that way, Mona," said Swamiji. "But until we know the Truth, our perception of what is good or bad may be erroneous. That is why the Prince told Murli, 'Have faith, and do not make judgments based on your perception of what is good or bad. One day you will understand the profoundness of Universal Wisdom. Have faith.'"

Swamiji continued.

> Murli deeply respected the Prince, but he had heard enough of his philosophy. "I don't think we should travel in the wilderness anymore," Murli said. "There is much in the civilized world that we can explore. I am not able to withstand any further profoundness of your Universal Wisdom."

"That should have brought an end to the Prince's wild goose chases," grinned Marcie.

"On the contrary," said Swamiji.

As soon as the Prince regained his health, he eagerly began his next trip with Murli in tow, venturing even farther from his father's palace. Only this time, their excitement of seeing new surroundings distracted them from properly recording the distance and direction of their journey. The Prince and Murli did not realize it, but they had crossed over the boundaries of their kingdom and had entered a prohibited and dangerous territory of an old and uncivilized tribe known for brutal activities, including torture and death.

Coincidentally, the chief of this uncivilized tribe was passing through with his entire entourage when one of the tribesmen saw the handsome Prince and his companion. He immediately told his chief about them and inquired if he could capture them in the light of their annual Ooaalaa celebration that was about to begin.

Swamiji's tone became more serious.

The highlight of their annual celebration was the sacrifice of a human being to please their Lord, Ooaalaa. Legend had it that the more handsome the human being they sacrificed, the greater their Lord would be pleased. The tribe's chief was thrilled to hear of the handsome man and immediately ordered his capture.

Swamiji paused to sip his tea, but realized his cup was empty. Anju immediately went into the kitchen and said, "Please wait for me Swamiji, I don't want to miss a thing!"

As they waited Manny decided that this was a good opportunity to ask the obvious question, "This isn't a true story, is it?"

Swamiji responded, "Manny, we are talking about *perceived* truth and *real* truth, and both are present in this story. It is entirely up to each of us to recognize which is which."

Manny was amazed how Swamiji had answered the question honestly and completely, yet he still did not understand the reply to his simple question.

Hearing some conversation from the other room, Anju called from the kitchen in a playful manner, "No cheating out there, Swamiji. You promised to wait for me. I'll be right there."

Anju's love and respect for Swamiji were obvious. In another moment, she returned with a tray full of tea and cookies. "Did I miss anything?" she asked. "Tell me the truth."

"Since you want us to tell you the truth," Susie teased her, "the truth is what we are trying to understand, aren't we, Swamiji?"

"You are very good with words, Susie," Swamiji replied. "Yes, truth is what we are hoping to unveil through this story. The *real* truth."

While Anju refilled everyone's teacup and passed around the cookies, Swamiji briefly closed his eyes, then resumed the tale...

> Engrossed in the awesome beauty of the surroundings, the Prince offered no resistance to the tribesmen capturing him and Murli. When they were presented to the the tribe's leader, the chief was very happy and proclaimed loudly, "This time, Lord Ooaalaa will be pleased with our sacrifice."

Although the Prince realized what was about to happen, he remained calm. But Murli was terrified and began crying almost uncontrollably. The tribesmen led them into a cave with no windows and only one entrance secured by guards. Murli could not bear the thought of the Prince's death, and perhaps his own. He became exhausted with fear and worry. Prince Mehar smiled at his friend and said, "Please do not be afraid, Murli. Have faith in the wisdom of the Universe. Things are not always as bad as they seem."

By this time, Murli was not in the mood to listen to more of the Prince's philosophy. He told him, "Please forgive me for being blunt, Sir, but we have heard stories about this tribe, and you know that they are brutal and merciless warriors. We are both facing certain death. How can you calmly talk about this so-called Universal Wisdom? I do not know how Universal Wisdom can help us now."

Then Murli became more hysterical, and began slapping the side of his head with his hands. "Oh, my Prince, I have failed to keep you safe and I am afraid to face my own death. Who will take care of my little daughter if I am dead? Oh sir, can't you do something?"

Murli looked at the Prince and was surprised to see him smiling, as if he were watching a humorous performance on a stage. Prince Mehar said, "My good and loyal friend, Nature has its ways. There must be a reason for all of this, so have faith and accept the Universal Wisdom. We need to remain calm and everything will be fine."

Unconcerned about the apparent crisis at hand, the Prince realized that the day's travels had made him very hungry. He asked his assistant, "Do you have anything to eat?"

"How can you think of food at a time like this?" Murli screamed back at him. He was trying to stay calm, but when he heard the Prince ask about food, he could not control himself any longer.

Suddenly the door of the cave opened, and four tribesmen appeared. Two of them appeared to be guards, as they were extremely well built and carrying weapons. The other two were carrying trays of food.

One of the guards said, "You are guests of our tribe tonight, and you will be served the very best food we can offer. If there is anything else that you desire, please let us know. Knock on the door as we are just outside." With that, the guard bowed and left the cave.

The Prince smiled at Murli and said, "See, I told you to have faith, and the powers and laws of the Universe will take care of us. Look at this delicious food they have prepared for us! I am starving! Let's eat!"

Murli looked at Prince Mehar in total amazement. He wondered if the Prince realized that they had just been given their ceremonial last meal. Murli was too nervous and worried to eat anything, and he just could not understand how the Prince was ready to eat with such enthusiasm.

Even though Murli had not spoken, the Prince understood what he was thinking. With a comforting smile he explained, "Universal Wisdom teaches us to live only in the now, rather than worrying about tomorrow or living imprisoned in our yesterdays. Losing ourselves in the past or the future will not change anything, but will only reduce our presence of mind.

"My dear Murli, it is only when we live in the present that our full capabilities and our natural intelligence are available to us, including our ability to think our way through challenging situations. Our full natural intelligence and total capabilities are only available to us when we operate in the now."

Sensing that Murli was beginning to feel better, the Prince said to him, "When one door is closed to you in life, another door is always opened, and often it is a wider door than before.

"Losing yourself
in the past or the future
will not change anything,
but will only reduce
your presence of mind."

But your chance to find that new door strictly depends on your faith that it exists and your persistence to search for it."

"But there is no door or even the smallest window for our escape," Murli replied. "How do you know where to look?"

Murli desperately wanted to share the Prince's faith.

"My dear friend," the Prince answered, "if you were to lose a tiny precious stone in a barn full of hay, would you search until you found it?"

"Of course I would," replied Murli. "If I knew that it was there, I would need to be patient, devise a plan, and then search until I uncovered it."

The Prince took Murli in his arms and gave him a big hug. "Then this is what we must do to find our diamond. Do not worry, my friend; everything will be all right. Let us have some food. It will give our bodies strength and help us to think more clearly."

Somehow Murli found himself feeling better and more hopeful although death was still hanging over their heads. His feelings of amazement had now become feelings of deeper admiration for the Prince and his faith, and he now recalled several situations where his Prince had come successfully through what initially appeared to be hopeless conditions.

Both men ate all they could, and soon fell into a deep sleep.

The screeching noise of the door woke them up the following morning. One of the men came forward and told them, "We only need one of you to sacrifice to our Lord." Then pointing to the Prince, he continued, "and our chief has chosen you. Come with us. We need to prepare you for our sacred ritual."

"Was Murli relieved when that happened, or did this upset him even more?" asked Susie.

"Murli was even more devastated," Swamiji answered. "Now that his mind was no longer clouded by concern for his own life, he realized that he was about to lose the Prince whom he adored and who was his anchor in life. This realization caused his heart excruciating pain, and he knew that it would only be relieved if he would give his own life in place of the Prince's."

"What a brave and loyal friend to make such a sacrifice," said Anju, with newfound respect for Murli.

Swamiji smiled and looked lovingly at Anju. "It is actually more difficult to bear the pain endured by others whom you love than to bear your own pain. When you are blessed to become a mother, Anju, you will learn this great lesson of life.

"You see, even in our day-to-day living, we only think more highly of ourselves when we selflessly make a difference in the life of another. This is true even when it causes us physical pain and hardship, and especially when there is no thought of recognition or rewards."

Anju realized that Swamiji had responded to her worldly question at a much higher level, and was astonished at the wisdom of his words.

In the space of a breath Swamiji turned again to his tale...

> Murli made a request to the lead tribesman, "Please, sir, take me instead. I am just as healthy and strong as he."

"We only think more
highly of ourselves
when we selflessly
make a difference
in the life of another."

The tribesmen did not know what their chief would say. They decided to prepare both of them for sacrifice so the chief could decide at a later time. As they started bathing the Prince, one of the men noticed that there was a stub and deep scar in place of one of his toes.

When the tribesman overseeing the preparation noticed this, he said, "We cannot use this man for our sacred sacrifice. He is not complete. Our Lord will be displeased and not accept him."

When the lead tribesman said this, Prince Mehar whispered in Murli's ear, "See? I told you that Nature had a reason for me to lose my toe. It has saved my life. Now, have faith in the Universal Wisdom and trust me. You, too, will be saved."

The men then examined Murli, and found that he had no scars or defects. They notified the chief that he was perfect for the sacrifice.

Patty sighed and said, "Murli should have been more careful. Sometimes, you get what you wish for."

"That is why we should never ask for things," said Swamiji. "We should simply learn the art of playing the game of life through a mindset of acceptance with gratitude for whatever happens."

"So what happened?" asked Ron. "Was Murli sacrificed, or was he saved, too?"

"Actually, Ron," Swamiji smiled, "the amazing thing is that Murli was sacrificed but his life was saved."

Everyone was puzzled by Swamiji's response. How could Murli be sacrificed and at the same time, be saved?

Swamiji sensed the confusion in the room and said, "The answer to this obvious contradiction is hidden within the story. Please allow me to continue."

> Prince Mehar was released and told that he was free to go. The Prince thanked the chief for his freedom and complimented him on conducting such an auspicious ceremony to please their Lord, in accordance with the manuscript left by the tribe's forefathers.
>
> Surprised and impressed by the Prince's knowledge of the sacrifice's meaning, the chief invited him to stay and sit at his side

"We should simply learn
the art of playing
the game of life
through a mindset
of acceptance
with gratitude
for whatever happens."

to watch the ceremony. Having established some level of confidence, the Prince asked the chief if he might offer some suggestions that would elevate the entire sacrifice ritual.

The chief grew suspicious and told the Prince, "If you are trying to trick me in order to save your friend's life, it will not work. It is our tribe's most treasured ceremony that we sacrifice a human being."

The Prince responded calmly, "Chief, I know that it is only through your kindness that I have been released. I do not mean to show any disrespect or anger you. I fully realize that a human sacrifice is the ultimate gift that can be offered to one's Lord. But, sir, I also know that if this sacrifice is *not* done correctly, your Lord could be immensely displeased and that could result in a curse on you and your tribe."

The chief did not expect the Prince to respond as he did and was at a loss for words. Prince Mehar continued, "I understand that you have faithfully conducted a ceremony and sacrifice every year."

The chief nodded.

"I truly am afraid that your Lord has not been pleased with your sacrifices and may be growing very upset with you. If you do not please your Lord this year, I fear what may happen to you and your people."

Hearing this, the chief became outraged and shouted at the Prince, "How dare you question my integrity!"

In a very soft tone the Prince explained, "Sir, please allow me to remind you what happened last year. Although you conducted this ceremony and sacrificed a very fine human being, your people still suffered a terrible famine. Thousands in your tribe starved to death, including innocent women and children.

"The year before," the Prince continued, "your tribe was affected by a horrible disease and you again lost many tribesmen, including some of your strongest warriors."

The chief was amazed that this stranger possessed such intimate knowledge. He demanded an answer from him.

"How do you know all of this?" the chief roared.

Prince Mehar knew the truth as he was regularly briefed about everything that happened in and around his kingdom. Although he did not know who the sacrifices were, he knew that they had been the most perfect persons the chief could find.

Before the Prince could respond, the chief demanded another answer, "Tell me, what are we doing wrong?"

The Prince replied, "Sir, chief, despite your most sincere and best efforts, your Lord is displeased because you are not sacrificing a *human*. All you are offering him is a dead human body. Your Lord is not looking for a corpse but a true living human sacrifice."

The chief was infuriated. "Why do you talk in riddles? You speak nonsense! These are humans and we sacrifice them to our Lord. How can there be any other kind of human sacrifice? If you want me to spare your life, tell me what you really mean."

The monk paused for a moment then resumed, his eyes alight with a gentle intensity.

> Although the Prince knew that the chief could easily have him killed, he also knew that truth was on his side. Even more importantly, he knew that his destiny was ultimately determined by Universal Wisdom. The chief could not harm him if his destiny was to live. These beliefs gave him the courage to present the truth to the chief without worrying about the consequences.
>
> Prince Mehar began his explanation in a humble voice. "Sir, there is *perceived* truth and *real* truth. Almost all of what we believe to be truths are *perceived* and *not real* truth. We use our extremely limited human senses to gather data and then we try to determine what is real with our highly prejudiced emotions and knowledge. Very often, we complicate our decision-making because *we see what we want to see* and *hear what we want to hear* to satisfy what we think we want and need."

The chief tilted his head and slowly shook it, conveying that he had not fully understood what the Prince had said. But clearly, he was becoming mesmerized by this wise and gentle voice.

Seeing the effect of his meaningful words, Prince Mehar went on. "We have been created and placed on this earth in a human body, which is nothing more than a human uniform. Looking through this window of perceived reality, we mistake this human uniform as *us*, the *real* human," he explained. "The real truth is that the *real me* is neither man nor woman, neither young nor old, neither short nor tall. All these physical characteristics are associated with this human uniform, and definitely not the *real* us. The *true* human lives beneath this uniform and *in* this body."

Swamiji fell silent. His attentive audience allowed the Prince's powerful words to settle in their minds.

"The true human lives
beneath this uniform
and in this body."

At last, Tony spoke up. "Wow, I've never heard it from that angle before."

"Prince Mehar was very learned and enlightened." Swamiji replied. He then returned to his story.

> The chief was now listening with great interest. The Prince said, "When a person dies, the real human within us moves on, and the human uniform, the body, is left behind. You see, sir, our *perceived* truth is that the person is dead, and as proof, his dead body lies lifeless. The *real* truth is that the *real human* never dies."
>
> The Prince asked the chief, "Sir, do you know why it cannot die? Or let me ask, do you know who this real human is?"
>
> By now, the chief was totally engrossed in this new window of reality the Prince was offering. Curiously, he responded, "No, I do not know. Please tell me."
>
> Prince Mehar began to feel that he was taking control of the situation.
>
> "Before I answer," voiced the Prince, "would you allow me to respectfully ask a question that is personal to your tribe?"

The chief was not expecting such forwardness from a prisoner, yet he was intrigued by the young man's question.

Growing up in the kingdom, the Prince heard many stories of this tribe. Legend had it that their founding fathers were very spiritual and had left very specific guidelines for future generations to follow. The Prince wanted to know what the written guidelines were for the annual human sacrifice ritual. He was sure that the intentions of the spiritual founders could never have meant the actual killing of a person.

Prince Mehar asked, "Would you kindly share with me the sacred instructions left by your forefathers regarding your annual ritual of human sacrifice?"

The chief was shocked that this young man knew so much about his tribe and was hesitant to divulge anything more. Despite what the Prince had told him, the chief still believed that he was properly following the path of his forefathers.

Sensing the chief's hesitation, the Prince said, "Chief, it is no longer a matter of sparing my life. I am at your mercy and you can do away with me as you wish."

Prince Mehar took a deep breath and went on, "Your Excellency, don't you really need to know why your Lord is displeased with your tribe in spite of all these great human sacrifices each year? You know that times have been very harsh for your regime. There have even been attempts on your life."

Swamiji gazed at his listeners and continued.

By this time, the chief realized that this young man had a special wisdom about him. He also knew that the Prince had been correct about the misfortunes that his tribe had experienced and the dissension that was growing within. Although he had always been careful to follow the guidelines of the annual ritual, he also knew that he did not completely understand the written guidelines handed down by the founding fathers.

The tribal chief did not want to show his excitement to the Prince or to the members of his own tribe, but he was beginning to think that this young man, who appeared wise beyond his years, might help bring an end to his many years of anguish and frustration.

The chief stood up from his high seat and asked the Prince to follow him to his private quarters. Immediately, an entourage of servants and bodyguards followed them, but the chief told all of them to stay outside in order to give them privacy. He also told one of the servants to bring them some tea. Once inside, the chief asked the Prince to be seated and wait for him to return with the tribe's sacred scriptures.

In time, the chief appeared with a book that was wrapped tightly in what obviously was very old silk of rich green, a color which the Prince learned later had deep spiritual meaning to the tribe's ancestry. It appeared to him that the book had not been opened for a long time.

They were interrupted by a knock on the door, and a servant entered with a tray of tea and an assortment of fruit and nuts. The servant poured them each a cup of tea, and bowing to the chief, departed.

With incredible and meticulous care, the chief then began unwrapping the silk cloth. Prince Mehar watched in silence as the chief looked through each page of the frail hand-written manuscript with utter respect.

The chief said, "I have found a passage that might be of interest. It is written here: *In order to get the true blessing of our Lord, it is essential for the tribe to clearly understand the difference between* perceived truth *and* real truth."

The chief was clearly shocked to see the same words that the Prince had used only moments earlier.

As if the Prince had read the chief's mind, he responded, "These are not my words, nor do they belong to your founding fathers. You should not be surprised that all of us have somehow been inspired to use these same words to communicate this critical difference between the perceived truth and real truth."

Then the Prince asked, "Have you found the passage pertaining to the ritual of human sacrifice?"

"Here it is," whispered the chief. He read it aloud: "*In order to discover the real truth, each year the tribe must conduct a sacred ceremony of the spirit where false personal selves are sacrificed. The tribe must sacrifice one's personal self, the person that separates one's self from the real truth, our Lord, and his blessings.*"

There was a moment of silence before the chief spoke again, "It clearly calls for us to *sacrifice a person*. What are we doing wrong?"

"The human sacrifice that the manuscript refers to is that of the *false personal self* or the *person in you*," said Prince Mehar. "These sacrifices are not about killing a human body, but the sacrifice of the person in us, which is our *false* self-identity.

We express this identity erroneously as *I, Me, My* and *Mine*."

The chief seemed spellbound as he listened to the Prince's interpretation.

"Your forefathers knew that we must sacrifice these identities of I, Me, My and Mine, because they separate us from our own souls, which is where pure Universal Wisdom resides. In other words, throughout our life we let our egos, agendas and our own selves cause us to disconnect from our universe, its powers and its wisdom."

"So there is *no* human sacrifice?" the chief asked.

"Oh yes, there is the *greatest* human sacrifice," replied Prince Mehar. "We sacrifice our *false* personal self, which is our I, Me, My and Mine false identities. All that will be left within us is the *Bigger Universal Being*."

"But how does this relate to perceived truth and real truth?" the chief asked.

"Chief, Sir," began the Prince, "just as you understand that your people are all

"Our egos, agendas
and selfish motives
disconnect us from our
own universe, its powers,
and its wisdom."

part of the same tribe, and that members of all tribes are all part of one human race, it will be clearer when you first accept that we all are a part of this Bigger One. Once you accept this, then it is easy to comprehend the difference between perceived truth and real truth."

Prince Mehar continued, "The perceived truth is that we all are separate entities. In other words, you are separate and I am separate. Whereas the real truth is that there is only one, the Bigger One, and we are all an inseparable part of that Bigger One that we are here to *serve unconditionally*."

Swamiji took a sip of his tea.

The Prince said, "To understand this clearly we do not have to look any further than at our own human body.

"It consists of many parts, such as hands, legs, eyes, ears and so on. Each part looks totally different and performs uniquely specific functions. Yet, each part is an integral part of the body as a whole.

But, if any part is separated from the body, that part simply cannot exist."

"So you are saying that each person is like a part of a body?" asked the chief.

"Exactly!" exclaimed Prince Mehar. "And in order for our body parts to coexist harmoniously, each part must serve the others and the overall body without any personal agendas or conditions. Although each part has its own name and purpose, they all must sacrifice their separate identities in order to serve the whole body."

"Just as we must sacrifice our I, Me, My and Mine identities in order to serve our Common Universe?" suggested the chief.

"That's correct!" the Prince replied. "The *real* truth is that there is only one Universal Wisdom, and we all are an inseparable part of the one universe that we are here to serve.

"Your founding fathers have asked your tribe to sacrifice their separate selves by letting go of their self-serving hidden agendas and selfish motives," Prince Mehar said.

"These agendas and motives diminish us and may even harm those who are an integral part of our Bigger One. Once we look at life from the window of this *real* truth, all frustrations that evolve from our self-centered thinking simply disappear."

The chief thought for a moment. "How do I make this happen?"

Prince Mehar replied, "Sir, I can help you achieve this by teaching your people to make the kind of sacrifices your forefathers wanted, but you must realize that it will take time. It will require your personal commitment to see it through."

"Legend has it," Swamiji concluded, "that as soon as the chief ordered the release of Prince Mehar and Murli, it started to rain. It was the kind of rain that the tribe desperately needed to avoid another devastating famine. When this occurred, the chief knew that they were finally on the right path."

"We are all an inseparable
part of that Bigger One
that we are here
to serve unconditionally."

Swamiji took a deep breath and looked into the faces of those in the room.

They all found Swamiji's story to be deep and intriguing, especially Ron who had even made a few notes and questioned, "Swamiji, could you please explain all this in a simple, practical way? I'm not grasping the concept of false identities of I, Me, My and Mine."

"You are not alone, my friend," Swamiji said. "In the story, Murli asked Prince Mehar exactly the same question after the Prince told him what had happened in the chief's quarters."

> The Prince said to Murli, "Do you remem-ber the time of your daughter's birth when you were blessed with a little baby girl? You were happy and joyous because she was of your own blood and genes. She was given a feminine name and all your relatives came to see her. She was showered with the prettiest gifts and welcomed to the family because she was their own niece, cousin, granddaughter and blood relative.
>
> "My dear friend," the prince continued. "If you look beyond this human body, you

and your wife were given a beautiful gift, but you never realized the truth that the divine spirit of the child is neither male nor female and had no relationship with the worldly human body. The divine spirit is sent to have a human experience and the *real* soul does not have a gender or a color, or worldly relationships, except that it is part of the same divinity that is present in each one of us.

"Instead, we raise the child in void of the truth," Prince Mehar explained. "The child learns to think strictly in a human body mode and operate in a mentality of I, Me, My and Mine. It is in the human body mode that the child is subjected to all of the human emotions of insecurity, fear, frustration, pain and all of our short-lived pleasures and miseries. This resulting selfish mindset restricts and confines the human spirit with that of limitations and boundaries that are associated *only* with the human body and *not* the *real us*, the divine soul."

"The real soul does not
have a gender or a color,
or worldly relationships,
except that it is part
of the same divinity
present in each one of us."

Marcie was fascinated by the wisdom expressed through the story, but she still could not see how one could apply it in daily life.

"Swamiji," she said, "it all sounds wonderful, but how does one constantly live in this 'divine mode' when there are bills to pay, your boss is an egomaniac, your child is sick, and there are a million other factors that we have no control over?"

Swamiji thought for a moment before speaking. "I may not be able to answer this question to your total satisfaction, Marcie, because the complete and correct answer lies *within* you. You each must look *deep inside yourself,*" he said.

Swamiji continued in a soft tone, "What I *can* tell you, and this is critical for you to understand, is that we run our lives based on and controlled by our habits, either knowingly or unknowingly. Our thoughts and our actions are guided by these habits, and not by the *real* you that resides in your body.

"Although the real you is within each of us, a person is only known by the habits he or she keeps. A person is never good or bad, but people can definitely develop habits that can be classified as being good or bad," he said.

"Interestingly, habits can be called software that nature has implanted in us. It allows us to operate in an 'autopilot' mode. Once we develop a habit, for example, such as driving a car, we can drive without even thinking about it. Remembering that habits can be either good or bad," he reminded them, "we are capable of putting ourselves on 'autopilot' for both good and bad habits, sometimes without even realizing it.

"One of our most common habits is that we see everything from a human body perspective," Swamiji told his listeners. "This habit creates obstacles that prevent us from seeing and comprehending everything from the Universal Wisdom that we are all *part of One.*

"On our journey through life, we must work to develop a founding habit that allows us to think, see, plan, act and know the Truth, which is that we are all an integral part of the One Universe. This fundamental habit will then simply overpower and leave no room for any of our bad habits associated with operating in the human body mode and fueling our self-serving agendas and ego," he said.

"So how do we develop this founding habit to become one with the Universe?" asked Susie.

Swamiji smiled. "In order to develop this habit of operating in the universal mode, we must first understand and then align ourselves and our thoughts with the Psychology of the Universe."

"Please excuse me for interrupting, Swamiji," David said, "but how do we know what the Psychology of the Universe is?"

Swamiji noticeably focused his attention through a large window into David and Anju's backyard. "David," Swamiji remarked, "your yard, with all of its trees and flowers and grass, is so beautiful and typical of the beauty and order of our universe.

"There is much that we can learn from studying nature and the natural law. But to fully understand the Psychology of the Universe, we must return to our 'cup of TEA,' and look at the wisdom and the remaining message that is hidden in the letters E and A."

Everyone was anxious to unveil the remaining ingredients of this special TEA recipe. It was clear, their fascinating journey was just beginning.

"We run our lives based
on and controlled by our
habits, either knowingly
or unknowingly."

Chapter Three

Wisdom of the Letter 'E'

During the break, Anju served warm samosas, a traditional Indian appetizer, cold beverages and prepared a fresh pot of tea. Everyone was eager to begin learning about Swamiji's new term, 'Psychology of the Universe.'

Even Manny, who grew up in India and was well exposed to eastern mythologies and ancient scriptures, found himself struggling to guess what it could be all about. Before Swamiji could begin, Manny could not wait to ask, "Does this have anything to do with our past life, or 'karma,' as is often talked about in Eastern religions?"

"I assure you Manny, this thought process is totally non-religious, and it has nothing to do with Eastern or Western philosophies," Swamiji replied.

"This is Universal Wisdom which remains the same no matter whether you are from the East or West."

Swamiji took a deep breath and looked around at each of the guests before he spoke again. "One of the main causes of our frustration is hidden in the second letter E of our special TEA recipe. I am sure you have guessed it by now. The letter E stands for expectations...our *erroneous* expectations," he said.

"If we honestly examine our lives, we will find that they are filled with expectations. We erroneously expect great things from our lives, our families, our friends, our society and from ourselves. Whether we know it or not, these expectations are usually self-centered and self-serving. It is when these expectations are not met that we become frustrated and disgusted with our lives and everyone around us."

Because of her experiences as an attorney, Marcie was not convinced that this thought process was practical and applicable in real life. She said, "Swamiji, we need to have expectations and set goals. Businesses cannot survive without planning and setting goals, or having expectations. In fact, the most successful motivational business gurus preach that you must have higher expectations for yourself, your employees, and even for your children in order for them to grow and achieve greater success."

A smile came to Swamiji's face. "Fundamentally, there is nothing wrong with setting goals or having expectations," he said, "as long as we realize that these are nothing more than techniques or instruments that point us in a certain direction.

"Often times," he continued, "we get so tense worrying about expected outcomes that we forget to focus on our responsibilities towards our real mission, the project or the game itself. Thus, our misdirected focus limits us from giving all of our intensity and concentration to the present, which is critically essential to achieving our mission and objectives.

"Universal Wisdom guides every aspect and component in our world. It begs us to always operate in the present, rather then getting lost in our expectations that are focused on the future. By focusing on the present, or in the *now* mode, we maintain our total concentration on the project at hand, rather then worrying about its future outcome.

"Moreover, operating in the *now* keeps us in a mode of creativity and thus, in alignment with the wisdom and the resources of the universe. It is in this creative mode that we remain stress-free and experience the elevation of joy within us. It is also in the creative mode that we are filled with positive energy."

"We get so tense worrying about expected outcomes that we forget to focus on our responsibilities."

"This sounds too good to be true," replied David.

"David, let me draw your attention to the game of football," replied Swamiji. "How often have you seen a very good team lose to a mediocre one? The better team plays with a focus not to lose, rather than letting their natural talent play a worry-free game.

"The better team is expected to win and as such, they let their expectations control them. They become stressed and frustrated with each mistake they make and in the end, they ultimately lose the game. The mediocre team, however, plays the game *without* any expectations. They simply *play for the moment* with all of their intensity and concentrated focus on each play. As a result, they win the game."

David and Manny looked at each other and nodded their heads in agreement, recalling many games in which Swamiji's example rang true.

"Goals and expectations generally have a primary focus," said Swamiji. "If this focus is simply to *benefit oneself* under all circumstances, without any consideration for others, therein lies the foundation for our frustration and stress. In such situations we would be operating *against* the Psychology of the Universe, and would have very little support from the universal forces within ourselves and outside of ourselves."

Anju had tremendous faith in Swamiji's wisdom but thought he was going a little too fast.

"Swamiji," she said, "please pardon me for interrupting, but before you go further with the 'Psychology of the Universe,' can you please go back and explain what you mean by 'erroneous expectations?' Are there any expectations that are not erroneous and are proper to have?"

Swamiji smiled and replied, "When our expectations are centered around our selfish agendas and do not add any benefit to others and our Bigger One, they are erroneous expectations. To fully recognize and comprehend the difference between our right and wrong expectations, please allow me to share a personal incident with you."

Swamiji looked down and thought for a moment, "Once I needed to put a nail in the wall, but I could not find a hammer. The best that I could find was a pair of pliers that had a fairly large surface area. I thought I could use it like a hammer. I tried to pound the nail into the wall with the pliers, but it did not work as I expected. I was hitting everything but the nail. I soon became very frustrated...do you know why?" he asked. "It was because I simply did not have the right tool for the job.

"Similarly, during our short journey on earth we are given a human system as our ultimate tool. This tool, of course, is not like a hammer or pliers. It is an incredibly sophisticated machine and most of its functions are fully automated. Most amazingly, it is designed to sustain itself and rebuild itself as needed.

"There is no question about this tool's capability," Swamiji asserted. "However, the question remains, 'What is the human system best designed for?' If we do not know the true purpose and understand its capabilities and limitations, we are going to misuse this tool, and doing so will result in unnecessary stress and frustration."

Swamiji glanced into the eyes of his guests. "The key element that we need to understand about our human system is that we are not the ones who designed it. Although a child is conceived and given birth through a human system, this only happens under very rigid Universal Laws.

"We hold our advances in science and technology in high esteem as we improve our society by curing diseases, implanting a human organ, flying a jumbo jet, designing a super computer, or sending a spaceship to Mars," he said. "These amazing advancements were developed by the human race only because we came to understand the exact nature of Universal Laws.

"One simple example of a Universal Law is that water always boils at one exact temperature under a given set of conditions, such as atmospheric pressure or the presence of impurities."

Swamiji continued, "To understand the intended design of our human system, we must first comprehend the underlying 'Psychology of the Universe.' This thought process is reflected in everything that nature has created. To understand it, we need to observe how nature works within us and all around us."

Swamiji got up from his chair and started walking towards the bay window in the family room. He smiled looking through the window and said, "Nature is a beautiful and silent reminder of the Psychology of the Universe."

He then pointed to a large apple tree in the middle of the yard. "May I invite everyone to look at this apple tree with a critical eye?" he continued. "This tree is a living example of nature's underlying thought process of unconditional serving.

"Many years ago when this tree was first planted,

it was probably a seed, or a tiny plant. It tolerated years of rain and storms and heat and cold to reach the stage it is in today. When it bears fruit, it has achieved its mission and we call it a successful apple tree.

"We also know that this apple tree was expected to reach this successful stage the very moment that its seed was planted, providing that no unusual event occurred, such as someone chopping it down. The intelligence or wisdom that was naturally present in the apple seed directed every one of the tree's characteristics, such as the shape of its leaves or the kind of apple it bears. It was all controlled by Universal Laws."

Curiously, David asked, "Swamiji, I agree that apple trees are a wonderful part of nature, but how exactly do they relate to the Psychology of the Universe?"

Swamiji smiled and replied, "To get an insight into the Psychology of the Universe, let us make another important but basic observation.

"Please allow me to ask a simple question. Has anyone ever seen an apple tree eat its own apples? Or has anyone seen an apple tree refuse to allow someone to pick its fruit? We know that the apples are the success the apple tree has achieved. Therefore, shouldn't the apple tree hold on to its success for itself?"

"It does not have a brain, Swamiji. It is just a plant," Manny answered. "It cannot think for itself, so it doesn't know how to make use of its own successes."

"Precisely, Manny," Swamiji replied. "In the absence of its own brain, which could have made it self-centered, the tree is controlled only by the laws of nature and guided by the Psychology of the Universe," he said. "The Psychology of the Universe guides everything around us and within us, including our thoughts and actions, providing our brain has not become contaminated by erroneous data such as our fear, greed, ego and other insecurities."

"But how can you compare the apple tree to our human body?" Manny asked.

"You can see the Psychology of the Universe even in our own body, Manny. If you examine the scientific composition of the human body, you will find that it is made up of zillions of tiny living cells," Swamiji pointed out. "These cells serve the body without any selfish agendas of their own. Many times they even sacrifice their very own existence to save the body from harmful and nasty diseases."

Swamiji's voice became soft and serious as he continued, "But once in a while, a cell comes along in our body that has its own agenda. This cell multiplies and grows, even at the cost of the very body that it exists within. My friends, we call this selfish cell a *cancer* cell."

There was absolute silence as the audience absorbed the impact of Swamiji's words.

"Astounding!" exclaimed Mona. "In all my years of medical schooling and practice I've never heard anyone explain cancer quite like that. But that's correct, Swamiji. Cancer does indeed cause such havoc within the body."

Ron nodded his head in agreement.

"And what's terribly sad," Mona continued, "is that when our most advanced treatments try to destroy the cancer cells, we end up destroying thousands and thousands of good cells in the process."

Swamiji replied, "This is also true, Mona, in our worldly body — our society. Terrorism acts just like a cancer cell that has its own selfish agenda. It acts contrary to the peaceful agenda of our worldly body. Unfortunately, in the process of fighting the cancer of terrorism, thousands of innocent, good lives are needlessly sacrificed, and our entire society pays a horrific price for the erroneous, self-centered agenda of a few cancerous individuals."

Once again, silence befell the room as these simple words explained the tragedies that everyone was witnessing in the news.

Marcie broke the silence with a question. "Swamiji, I certainly am not advocating terrorism or cancer, but don't we have a responsibility to stand up for what we believe in, and to *first* take care of ourselves in this world?"

Swamiji responded, "The Psychology of the Universe is founded on the Universal Truth, where everything is part of One. Therefore, everything in its inherent nature must serve this Bigger One. This only fails to occur when we are influenced and contaminated by factors which are contrary to thinking as One, such as my personal agenda and worrying about myself, even at the cost of others.

"When we think independently with self-centered, biased and faulty data, and we ignore the truth of being One, we end up going against the basic Psychology of the Universe. Unknowingly, we become self-serving just like the cancer cell."

Tony broke his silence and said, "Are you saying that even our human system is designed to follow the same Psychology of the Universe and serve the Bigger One?"

"When we think
with self-centered bias
and we ignore the truth
of being One...
unknowingly, we become
self-serving just like
the cancer cell."

Swamiji looked at Tony and said, "Our human system follows the same Psychology of the Universe, except that our human body is given its own independent brain to think, choose and act. When we operate in alignment with how our human system was designed, and when we think and use our brains to enhance our human capacity to serve the Bigger One unconditionally, we will experience enormous joy in our hearts.

"There are times when our brain becomes contaminated with erroneous data," Swamiji continued, "and then we think and act in conflict with the way that our human system was designed. It is under these circumstances that we become self-centered, and we then experience stress and frustration. The difficult part to understand is that we must not lose sight that *we ourselves are part* of the Bigger One. Once we lose our self-identity of I, Me, My and Mine, we begin to see even our own human system as a simple part of the Bigger One and we begin to serve our own selves unconditionally.

"We must always remember," he said, "that we ourselves are a tool designed in the form of a human system. This human tool has been designed only to serve the Bigger One by adding value to it, and never by subtracting value from it. The brain acts as our human system's computer that is supposed to help us achieve our true mission of constantly and creatively enhancing our value-adding capabilities. Therefore, it is critical that we must always operate in the true student paradigm."

"This sounds wonderful," agreed Susie. "But isn't it very hard on us to always have to worry about adding value?"

"When we practice this thought process uncon-ditionally, Susie, it is truly very rewarding and stimulating," replied Swamiji. "It is when we misuse this human tool, by not performing as we are designed, that we experience stress and frustration. Our self-serving and selfish thinking leads us to *erroneous expectations* and results in our frustrations."

Susie was engrossed in this newfound reality. "Swamiji, I have always believed in goal setting, and I have a lot of goals. Is that wrong?"

Swamiji smiled and answered, "As we said earlier, goals are often part of our expectations. When we set goals, they are often designed to benefit us, so we can receive rewards such as fame, wealth and pleasure. We often have no consideration for the goals' effect on the Bigger One, and sometimes we set these goals even to the detriment of the Bigger One. My friends, when the direction of my goals and expectations are towards 'myself,' without adding value or providing benefit to others in our society, we will undoubtedly experience stress and frustration.

"On the other hand," said Swamiji, "if we set our goals so that their outcomes create benefits to others, we will then be in alignment with the Psychology of the Universe. This mindset allows us to operate within the design capacity of our human tool, and will lead to our peak performance. The most amazing thing," he said with emphasis, "is that when our goals and expectations are in alignment with the wisdom of the Psychology of the Universe, not only are we less stressed and frustrated, but we also are in a position to achieve incredible worldly success."

A well-read student of autobiographies of famous achievers, Tony suddenly realized the profound link between the stunning successes of these leaders and the thought process Swamiji had just shared with them.

Before Tony could comment, Patty jumped in.

"Where do our families fit into all of this, Swamiji?" she asked. "Is it wrong to have positive expectations and plan for the well-being of our families?"

"When the direction
of my goals
and expectations
are towards 'myself,'
without adding value
to others, we will
undoubtedly experience
stress and frustration."

"Your question appears to be valid, Patty," Swamiji replied in a mild but firm tone. "That is, until we realize that this concern comes from our old way of thinking of individuality and personal ownership. It fails to take into account that we are an *inseparable* part of the Bigger One.

"Just as you must always remember that you, yourself, are part of the Bigger One, so you must also always bear in mind that your family is part of the same One. Your concern for their welfare must be in compliance with developing their role to ultimately serve the Bigger One. Your responsibility is to serve your family, so that their abilities have been enhanced to do so. Thus, our mindset must always be to serve the Bigger One, whether we are serving ourselves, our family, our friends and neighbors, or our society."

Gauging the response among his listeners, Swamiji moved on, "There is a very specific detail that is vital to understand to fully implement this thought process. If we use our human body again as an example, we know that it consists of many individual parts. If we should encounter a serious accident that injures many of these parts, including some of our vital organs, what will the doctors look at first when we get emergency treatment? They will first read your vital signs, because saving your life is more critical than saving your parts.

"Therefore, your broken hand and ankle will be taken care of much later, only after your vital signs are brought under control. In that same light, the vital signs of our bigger society must be stabilized first before we can begin taking care of the individuals within the society," Swamiji emphasized.

"You see, when we think in terms of I, Me, My and Mine, and when we erroneously express our ownership as being my family, my body, my health, my spouse, my job or my anything…we are separating ourselves from the Bigger One."

Swamiji noticed that Marcie was shaking her head, conveying that she was not buying into this thought process.

Attempting to clarify his words, Swamiji continued, "Please allow me to share my observations of our worldly successes. The most amazing fact is that we are *designed* to operate in this thought process, and we don't even realize it."

Swamiji smiled and said, "Take, for example, our friend and esteemed neurosurgeon Dr. Ron Smith. I am sure that when he is in the act of operating on a patient, he does not worry about the fee, or any personal or family issues. I can assure you that his entire concentration during the operation is focused on *saving his patient's life.* In addition to himself, his team of professionals is also totally focused on achieving that same objective, even when the operation lasts eight or ten hours. Yet Ron and his team are so totally engrossed in the operation that they lose all sense of time and are unaware of their personal fatigue. The thrill of a successful operation and saving a life has displaced thoughts of money and other rewards, as well as any self-centered concerns."

Everyone nodded in agreement. Ron smiled and admitted that many times his operations would continue nonstop for up to 12 hours. It was beyond his comprehension that he was always able to perform such surgeries and still feel great afterwards, providing that he had been able to save his patient's life.

Then Swamiji pointed a question towards Manny, "Even in business, the real success comes from *adding value* to your customers. Isn't that right?"

"Oh my, you just gave me the answer to a big dilemma I am facing, Swamiji," Manny replied. "Yes, it really makes sense."

Manny was thinking about the powerful marketing agency that he had hired to help market a new concept his team had developed, but all the fancy tools developed by the agency were not showing any results in his bottom line. Manny realized that his company's new concept was not designed with a mindset to add value to his customers, but to reduce costs and increase profits. Manny also realized that the products that brought him previous successes had always been designed adding the highest value to the customer.

Still looking at Manny, Swamiji remarked, "All of our innovation, our intelligence and our fancy marketing skills will not produce favorable results, especially in the long run, if the products and services we offer fail to add value to the buyer, and to our overall society.

"Furthermore, to be a long-term success, it is not enough to just add value. We must focus on continuous improvement and work towards adding the *highest value* in our field. There is no room for mediocrity in this thought process," Swamiji smiled. "We must also realize that all of our inner strength comes from being truthful. The real truth is that we are One. This truth must always be present, because in its absence, all that we will have is dishonesty."

Tony could not contain his amazement at the wisdom of these words. "Simply amazing! This is so simple, yet so profound! No wonder why we miss it most of the time. This fundamental realization gets overlooked because we get lost in the phony glamour of today's world," Tony said.

"That is absolutely right, Tony," Swamiji agreed. "There is another fact about human beings that we must face, otherwise we will never be able to gain our sanity, our real security and our inner confidence. The fact is that we may be able to fool the entire world around us, but we will never be able to fool our *inner* self. Whenever we work towards goals and have expectations which are self-centered and self-oriented, our opinion of ourselves does not get enhanced. In fact, we even think less of ourselves. It is only when we provide selfless service and set goals that benefit others, that we think more highly of ourselves."

"But Swamiji," said Marcie, "we always see people with worldly successes and, regardless of how they achieved them, they are very confident and secure. I know some of these people personally, and I can tell you that they have not made their name by adding value to society. They only think of themselves. In fact, they are proud of how smart they are, and they try to teach others that this self-centered approach is the way for others to also obtain success! This inner self that you have been talking about, I don't think it exists in them."

"We may be able
to fool the entire world
around us, but we
will never be able
to fool our inner self."

Marcie knew in her heart that Swamiji's words were true, but she was frustrated trying to understand how they would fit into the real world that she lived in and with the real people she dealt with every day.

Swamiji considered his next words for a moment and said, "Things are not always as they appear, Marcie. You have only seen the outside appearance of these people, but you have never been exposed to the turmoil that exists within them. You see, there are two types of confidence. One is *pseudo* confidence, and the other is *real* confidence. Pseudo confidence requires crutches such as titles, possessions, money, trophies and other worldly accomplishments that certify in our own minds that we are superior in some way. The moment that these crutches are taken away, our confidence drops, and we feel utterly depressed. Some people plummet into a despondent state of mind and even become suicidal."

Swamiji took a deep breath and said, "We must always remember that real confidence only comes from our inner endorsement of our activities, which are in full compliance with the Psychology of the Universe. Amazingly, this real confidence sets us free from needing any worldly crutches, such as titles, trophies and money, and we are filled with joy and contentment."

"Are you saying, Swamiji, that having worldly possessions or fame is bad?" Marcie asked.

Swamiji smiled gently and said, "My friends, all these worldly crutches that give us pseudo-confidence are neither bad nor good. It all depends on how we use them. Please let me share a story with you that may clarify what I am trying to say."

On hearing these words, Anju sat up attentively. From the very first time she had heard Swamiji speak when she was a young girl, she had always loved his insightful stories. His wise words were always spoken in a simple way that she could somehow relate to and apply in her daily life.

With enthusiasm in his voice, Swamiji began.

There was a young lad named Steven who was very athletic and disciplined. Steven wanted to use his talents to earn a name for himself through athletic competition. Having tremendous interest in swimming, his school coach encouraged him to focus all his attention on competing in regional and national swim meets. Steven worked very

"Real confidence
comes from our
inner endorsement
of our activities
that are in full compliance
with the Psychology
of the Universe."

hard and won several prestigious trophies. He had become a world-class swimmer.

One day Steven's coach sat him down and told him that he believed he was capable of competing in the Olympic games. Excited at the possibility and the challenge, they found an Olympic trainer and gathered support from the school and various civic organizations to help fund his efforts. After many long months of diligent training, Steven and his coaches were encouraged that he was ready for the tryouts.

On the day of Olympic qualifications, Steven won many of the trials he competed in and easily made the team. Steven simply could not believe that he would represent his country among the world's greatest athletes. His nation's finest coaches told him to prepare to compete in several events, as they believed he was the team's best candidate to earn multiple medals.

As Steven's training intensified, he began to meet regularly with a psychologist who specialized in working with Olympians.

This psychologist instructed him to keep his focus in the present and not to get preoccupied with his expectations or his worries.

Finally, the Olympics arrived and Steven performed extremely well. All of his training and hard work paid off. When the games were over, he wore eight gold medals around his neck. His picture was on the front page of every major newspaper and cover of every magazine. He was the new national hero.

The sudden attention and the incredible opportunities he was being given awed Steven. He was only 18 years old and he did not really know anything else besides swimming, yet the most famous journalists and newscasters interviewed him. He was also invited to speak at major events across the country.

As time passed, however, Steven began to notice that his relevance to society was starting to decline. The demand for interviews, public appearances and speaking engagements at special events greatly diminished. Accordingly, his endorsement earnings also decreased. In the absence of the worldly crutches he had become accustomed to, Steven began to lose confidence in himself.

Sadly, in a relatively short period of time after the peak of his popularity, Steven's confidence was lost and he became very depressed. After all his years of dedication, unprecedented athletic achievements, fame and recognition, he simply could not understand how people could literally forget about him. He felt that people wouldn't notice or care if he lived or died.

"We do live in a cruel world, don't we?" Patty said with motherly feelings.

Swamiji looked at her with compassion. "What really happened to Steven is that he lost confidence in himself because he was relying on the support and endorsement of *others*, rather than finding true confidence *within*. He began to live in his own world of his perceived and self-created expectations," Swamiji emphasized. "Steven eventually became a victim of his own self-centered erroneous expectations because he did not operate in the present where he could have added value to his Bigger ONE, his society.

"You see," said Swamiji, "all of our worldly successes are only given to us in order to create a platform for us to add higher value to our society. All worldly successes are temporary, and if we fail to use these temporary grace periods to add value to others, then all of our fame and wealth lose their effectiveness and importance. Eventually, they become a burden in our life."

David was visibly intrigued by this notion. He said, "Swamiji, this is a very fascinating way to think, and I want to fully understand. It seems to me that Steven worked very hard for his success, and he deserved to win the medals and all the fame that came with them. What should he have done differently?"

"Steven had taken on and accomplished a mission to win in the Olympics," Swamiji replied. "After attaining his success, he was in a position to take on an even *greater* mission to add value to others. For example, he could have worked to open schools to train future athletes for the Olympics, or help orphan children gain an education, or he could have helped raise funds to find a cure for a terminal disease. If he would have adopted any of these new missions, Steven's name would have never been forgotten. He may have even become more popular," Swamiji pointed out.

"All of our worldly successes are only given to us in order to create a platform for us to add higher value to society."

"You see my friends," Swamiji continued, "each success helps us attain a new platform, as long as we remain focused on our true purpose of life — to continuously add the highest value to the Bigger One."

Marcie was still thinking about the many people she knew who had obtained great wealth, and commented, "But Swamiji, I know that some of the people who became wealthy and successful never considered adding the highest value. They continued to build success upon success, and became wealthy without caring about helping others."

"That is an excellent point, Marcie," said Swamiji, "and it allows me to clarify two important messages.

"First, there are many examples where people have had short-term success, strictly driven by self-centered motives, and without having concern for adding value to society. People may have bought their new product or service because it was a new fad or in style. But these are short-term worldly successes that only give temporary pseudo-confidence and are void of any endorsement within one's inner self.

"Secondly," he went on, "the Psychology of the Universe is all around us, and it is planted deep within our subconscious without our even knowing it. Sometimes decisions are made with selfish intentions, but they still result in adding value to others. When these results occur and they realize that they accidentally added this value, the people who made the original self-centered decision end up feeling some sense of accomplishment. This feeling is endorsed by their inner self, resulting in some measure of security and confidence."

"If I understand you correctly, you are not against making money or gaining fame, as long as in the process we add value to our society," remarked Susie.

"The critical distinction is in your primary focus," Swamiji agreed. "To stay in alignment with the natural wisdom of the universe, our primary focus must be to always serve the Bigger One by adding the highest value to it. This process gives us *real* success. As a by-product, we are placed in a position to gain the worldly success symbolized by wealth or fame, and along with this worldly success, we will then have the platform to add even higher value."

Swamiji paused for a moment and glanced at each of his listeners with a smile. "And that, my friends, is the secret of true success in this world."

Mona could not resist asking, "I understand what you have been saying, Swamiji. But how do we keep our focus on adding value when so many things happen in our lives that we have no control over? These unexpected events totally destroy our schedules and best laid plans to add value."

Swamiji grinned, "The answer to your question lies in the wisdom that is hidden in the letter A, the last letter of the word TEA."

Immediately the room filled with anxious curiosity, the last letter of the recipe was about to be told.

"To stay in alignment
with the universe,
our primary focus must
be to always add
the highest value."

Chapter Four

WISDOM OF THE LETTER 'A'

After a short break, David eagerly gathered his friends to continue the discussion.

Swamiji saw an earnest look in everyone's eyes waiting for him to unveil the wisdom hidden in the last letter of the word TEA. He asked, "Do you have any guesses on what our final letter A stands for and how it can help us minimize our frustrations?"

"I have been thinking about this during the break, Swamiji," said Susie. "Could it stand for anxiety or anger?"

"How about A standing for act like in acting this way?" suggested Anju.

"Those are all good suggestions," replied Swamiji, "but they will not make the best recipe for our TEA."

Then Manny volunteered, "If my mother were here, she would probably say acceptance. She always taught me to accept everything with grace and gratefulness."

"You have a very wise and perceptive mother, Manny," Swamiji said, quite impressed.

"Yes, the letter A in the word TEA stands for *acceptance*. This letter may be rather easy to guess, but it is hard to comprehend. And it is even more difficult to practice in real life.

"When something unexpected happens, we get upset. Often our first response is to look for a reason or person to blame rather than to creatively and calmly evaluate what can be done with the new situation. We do not understand the wisdom of accepting and moving forward to make the best of the situation.

"The natural wisdom of the acceptance paradigm teaches us that there is always a reason why things happen to us and around us. It is entirely up to us to find good opportunities in these situations and sincerely look for ways to add the highest value," he said. "The more gracefully we accept every situation, whether we perceive it as being good or bad, the better our chances will be to find a clear path to make a difference and add value."

"There is always a reason
why things happen...
it's entirely up to us
to find ways to add
the highest value."

"Swamiji, are you saying that whatever happens to us — wrong or right — we should simply accept it without questioning or investigating?" Marcie asked.

"On the contrary, Marcie," responded Swamiji. "When understood correctly, this thought process empowers us to take charge of the situation by first accepting it, without judging it to be right or wrong. Then, we can go *forward* with our full attention and creativity, having a well thought out action plan that is free of contaminants such as judgment, anger, remorse, greed, fear or ego."

"I am still confused," said Mona. "You must be talking about ideal or theoretical situations, right? I don't see how this could be practiced in the real world."

"Have you ever watched a professional card player?" Swamiji asked. "They do not complain about the cards they are dealt. They simply play with the cards they have in hand, and make the best of them, no matter whether the cards are good or bad. That is what the paradigm of acceptance really is.

"Let me share a real life story that happened with my very close friend, Tom Winters," Swamiji said gently. "I first met Tom when we were students at MIT. I was pursuing my master's in aeronautical engineering and he was studying electrical engineering. That must have been in the early seventies."

Everyone in the room was astounded to hear these words, and Ron gave voice to their wonder. "We didn't know you were educated in the States and that you're an aeronautical engineer from MIT to boot!"

Having an engineer's mindset himself, Tony said, "Swamiji, I just have to ask—what's the connection between your highly technical education and the philosophical wisdom that the world seeks in your lectures and seminars?"

An impish smile appeared on Swamiji's face, along with a twinkle in his eye. "At MIT they cooked my brains, thus I was left with no choice but to use my heart to express ordinary and simple thoughts. People have come to label this as 'philosophical wisdom.' But please allow me to continue telling you about my friend Tom. Fortunately, *his* brain remained intact even after being deep-fried by MIT."

With Swamiji's subtle humor, everyone's lingering look of hesitation turned to a smile.

"Tom was hardworking and honest," said Swamiji. "Highly innovative and creative, Tom was offered a very lucrative position with a medium-sized company after graduation. Working just outside of Boston, Tom was very happy with his new job and made tremendous contributions to the organization. Within only three years, Tom was rewarded with a vice-presidency position, growing the company ten-fold and making it extremely profitable.

"This was a privately held company with one individual owner. One day the owner received an offer to sell his company to a much larger corporation. The offer was handsome and one the owner could not refuse. The sale caught everyone by surprise," said Swamiji. "Soon, new management consolidated the company and eliminated several key positions. Despite all of his contributions, Tom was a victim of these changes. Suddenly, he found himself out of a job. He was devastated. Tom had worked very hard in building this business and loved his work.

"Lost as to what he would do next, Tom came to see me in New York City, where I was working at that time. I tried to calm him down, sharing with him the wisdom of the acceptance paradigm. I suggested that he look at this situation as an opportunity, as there is always one present, and many times opportunities are even better than the previous situation. Tom laughed and said that it was not possible to find a better opportunity than what he had at the job he lost.

"My friend was very depressed. Trying to cheer him up, I took him out for a big dinner at a well-known Italian restaurant. As we were waiting to be seated, a gentleman approached Tom and asked, 'You're Tom Winters, aren't you? I've been trying to contact you since I learned that your company had been sold. Do you remember me? I'm Jack Anderson, president of The Anderson Company.'

"Tom had recognized Jack right away, as it had been his direct responsibility to serve the Anderson account. It was Tom who had developed it into one of his former company's biggest customers. 'How could I not remember you, Mr. Anderson?' Tom replied. 'You were my favorite and largest account!'

"With a smile, Jack said, 'You know, I would like you to continue having Anderson as your favorite and largest customer.'

"Tom looked at Jack with great appreciation and said, 'I appreciate your faith in me, Mr. Anderson, but I guess you have not heard. I do not work there any more. With this buyout, my job was eliminated.'

"Jack grabbed Tom's hand, and said to him, 'I know that. That is why I want you to start your own company, and produce and supply Anderson with the same quality product, technical support and service that I have received from you before. I do not have much faith in the new ownership. They already have increased our price, and there have been delays in filling our orders.'

"Tom was absolutely wonderstruck and could not speak a word.

"Jack sensed his uncertainty and said, 'My friend, do not be concerned. I am willing to finance the entire deal. Then, I will recover my loan through discounts on our purchases over the course of our relationship.'

"Today, Tom is a multi-millionaire. He didn't realize it at the time his job was eliminated, but a tremendous opportunity was about to unfold for him that was far beyond his imagination."

Manny had been listening intently and began to speak as soon as Swamiji stopped. "You know, Swamiji, I can really relate to what happened to Tom. Being foreign-born and coming to this country with no credit history, it was extremely difficult for me to start and grow my business.

"One day I traveled to a remote area to meet with a potential investor," Manny said, "but he turned me down because he could not relate to the vision of my business. As I returned home feeling very depressed,

I passed a man who was standing beside his car along a country road."

Manny continued. "At first I felt that I should stop to help him, but then I told myself that I was much too busy and had my own problems, so I passed him by. My conscience kept asking me, 'What if that person was me, or someone I loved, and no one stopped to help?' I knew that I could not live with myself if I did not go back and help him. I turned the car around and went back.

"To try to make a long story short, the man had a flat tire, and he had been already riding on his spare. I gave him a ride to the nearest town, but then we ran into another problem. The small-town business did not accept the credit card he carried, and he did not have enough cash to buy a new tire. I ended up buying the tire for him, and then helped him change it.

"When the man asked me for my address so he could pay me back for the tire and give me something for my time and trouble, I answered in a way that surprised even me. Something inspired me to say, 'Sir, you can only pay this debt by helping the next stranger that you come across who needs your help. I only told him that my friends called me 'Manny' and he told me his name was 'Bob.'

"Two days later I was calling on a potential customer, and I was not having much success because they had a long relationship with their current supplier. The person I was talking to, however, said that he would talk to the company's president about my product. He realized that my product offered an upgrade from what they were currently buying. I asked him if I could meet his president and speak to him myself. Imagine my total shock when I saw that the man behind the president's desk was Bob, the man with the flat tire!

"Bob was a shrewd businessman," Manny recalled, "and he listened to my entire presentation. Then he said, 'I would like to make you my supplier, but it's not because you helped me with my tire. It's because you offer a superior product and I trust that you'll be a good business partner for us.' Then he gave me an order that floored me. It was a huge order that I did not have the capacity to produce."

Manny continued, "When I told him that I could not fill his order, he asked me what it would take for my company to produce that amount of product. I told him that it would take about a half-million dollar investment to do so. He then made me an offer that I will never forget. He said, 'Manny, I'll write you a check today for $500,000. I want a 20% discount off your best price, with 10% being credited towards my loan, and the other 10% being a special discount. When the loan is repaid, you will continue to give me this 10% discount throughout our relationship.' And that's how my business got started!"

"You never told me that, Manny," David said. "That's quite a story."

Swamiji smiled. "You see, Manny, the acceptance paradigm must be unconditional and without judgment. We must accept things without labeling them as good or bad, no matter how we perceive them. We always need to be of a mindset to find an opportunity to add value to every situation.

"There are many people who know they have great ideas that can add value, but they are insecure and unwilling to take risks," said Swamiji. "When they encounter difficulties, or sometimes even when they encounter unexpected but positive opportunities, they give up, depriving society and themselves of the benefits of their unfulfilled creativity.

"All creativity comes *through* us. We are a conduit to the Universal Wisdom. It is only through us that the Universe can deliver all the gifts of its talents and resources that we may use to serve the Bigger One. We must always accept the responsibilities of the situations that we are placed in."

"We are a conduit
to the Universal Wisdom."

Manny leaned forward as if drawn into this profound idea.

Swamiji continued, "There is another fact of life that we all need to make peace with. Regardless of how much power we have in terms of money, fame, political influence, strength or authority, many times we are simply unable to change the situation we are placed in. We have no alternative but to accept the situation," he said.

"The question then becomes whether we accept the situation with grace and without emotional scars, or whether we choose to become bitter and scarred for life. This decision is totally up to us."

Swamiji looked at Susie and Ron and said, "As young children, our wisdom is very limited to know what is really good for us. If, on a child's birthday the parent asks, 'What gift do you want?' the parent already knows what the child really needs and what would be best for the child, although the child might answer that he wants this toy or this game or that gadget. Even if the parent were to give the child something much *better* than what he had asked for, his initial reaction may be very negative: 'I don't want this!' The parents may try to justify the gift, saying 'This is better,' but the child will likely insist, 'No, no, I don't want this. I want what I asked for!'

"Whether we realize it or not," Swamiji said, "the same thing goes for each of us. Although we look like grownups, and even after we have children and grandchildren, our wisdom remains very limited. We cannot see far beyond our experiences and beyond what we have seen or come to know. As a result, we keep asking for the wrong things, and when we don't get what we ask for, we become upset.

"In contrast," he said, "how many of us have ever asked in our prayers, 'Please, Lord, I don't know *what* I want. I don't know what is good for me. Please help me experience the joy of life by giving me wisdom and the resources I can use to add the highest value to the Bigger One'?"

Hearing this, Swamiji's listeners were clearly affected by the implication of this simple prayer.

Swamiji wanted to reinforce the paradigm of acceptance, so he continued with a real-world example. "I personally witnessed the real power of the principle of acceptance in 1947 when old India was first divided into present-day India and Pakistan. Millions of people were forced to leave their homes and their belongings without notice and move into temporary shelters in completely unfamiliar surroundings. Making this tragedy even more difficult, many of these people also lost their loved ones during these unexpected and life-changing events.

"As difficult and devastating as this situation was, some of these people were somehow able to accept the situation. They immediately took charge of their lives. To survive, they put aside their former occupations and accomplishments and did whatever they could to get by," said Swamiji.

"These people experienced excruciating pain and tolerated immense hardship, but they learned to be innovative and creative. They improvised, changed their way of living and never gave up. They accepted the cards they had been dealt, and they managed every situation they were subjected to. Today, some of these people are India's most successful business and political leaders.

"Meanwhile," he said, "many others in the same situation simply could not let go of what happened to them and their families. They did not understand the wisdom of acceptance. They chose to become bitter, hostile, depressed and even suicidal.

"You see, my friends," Swamiji pointed out, "in life there are no guarantees. Often, life is not even a fair game. All that we have are our efforts, courage, ingenuity and our willingness to work hard at whatever opportunities are presented to us."

Swamiji looked to the group before him. "Once we know that our cause or objective is in full compliance with our mission of adding the highest value to our society, we become empowered, and at the same time capable of handling any worldly setbacks. The difference between failure and success is having the courage to accept temporary setbacks, learn from them and look for opportunities to achieve our real mission of adding the highest value."

Picking up his tea, Swamiji went on. "The amazing thing about the letter A is that contrary to how it may appear on the surface, acceptance also means that we should never give in to the finality of the failure itself. Viewed from the window of the acceptance paradigm, all failures, setbacks and tragedies are simply new opportunities."

David was fascinated with this last comment. He never imagined that acceptance could lead to new opportunities.

"Viewed from the window
of the acceptance paradigm,
all failures, setbacks
and tragedies are simply
new opportunities."

Swamiji sipped his tea and continued. "Let us take a look at another real-world example. We are all aware of dedicated scientists who spend their entire lives performing thousands of experiments in their mission to find a cure for some dreaded disease, such as cancer. They know that each experiment renders an outcome, and they use that outcome to build upon and perform future experiments.

"True scientists do not become discouraged when the outcome of the experiment does not meet their expectations," emphasized Swamiji. "They completely accept it and use the information as a knowledge base to plan for the future. If scientists were to become unhappy or frustrated and give up because the result of their experiments did not meet their expectations, they would never be able to achieve life-changing, Nobel Prize-winning inventions and discoveries.

"Likewise, what mother gives up on her child when she is teaching the child to walk? She knows that every time her baby stumbles, these temporary setbacks eventually will lead to the day when the child will be able to walk on his or her own."

"I never thought about it this way, Swamiji," Patty responded. "But you are right. Sometimes we thought David would never walk on his own, but he kept trying, and we kept picking him up."

Marcie was hearing Swamiji's words through her own experiences as an attorney, and wanted to share her perspective. "Swamiji, if injustice is done to you, should you simply accept it and do nothing about it? If we didn't fight for our civil rights in this country, we would still have slavery and gross injustice around us."

Swamiji thought for a moment and responded, "Our mission is to add the highest value to the Bigger One, unconditionally. Adding value can include fighting injustice or bringing about dramatic and positive changes in society. But, we must first *accept* and analyze the outcomes with total calmness. Otherwise," he said, "if we allow our emotions to control us, we can become angry and revengeful and that will infest us with hatred instead of the desire to add value.

"Hatred is like a cancer, which destroys the body that hosts it," Swamiji said emphatically. "It kills your ability to think objectively and creatively. If this happens, you may take radical and unwise steps that not only grossly disempower you, but also produce conflict and can eventually create disharmony in the entire society. Worse yet, this may start a chain reaction and long-term feuds that last for generations. In the most extreme cases, hatred is really at the very core of the terrorism that is paralyzing our world.

"To fully understand and practice the paradigm of acceptance we must separate ourselves from this *human* experience, the worldly *us*. This is like bringing into a game a neutral third party, such as a referee, who is emotionally unattached to the situation, and can think and act rationally. Once we separate ourselves from our emotions and accept the outcome of a situation without judgment," said Swamiji, "we become that neutral and rational third party within ourselves. This is an overwhelming accomplishment. This process leads to frustration-free thinking, acting and living in the present, with full access to nature's abundant resources on a moment-to-moment basis.

"This is why our society has professionals, like you, Marcie, whom we call attorneys, counselors or consultants. These professionals are supposed to remain free of emotion and provide rational thinking to us in times of difficulty and injustice. They first accept the facts about the current situation that no one can change. It is only after this total acceptance that they plan or advise on future action strategies."

Anju was listening attentively and said, "Swamiji, are you asking us to always refrain from being judgmental? Are we supposed to stay neutral, even if someone takes advantage of us, or deceives us, or purposely harms us? How can we accept such a situation?"

Swamiji smiled and closed his eyes for a moment, as if trying to find the right words to help everyone understand the empowering wisdom of acceptance.

He finally looked at Anju and said, "It would simply be impossible for us to understand or practice the paradigm of acceptance in absence of the first letter of the word TEA. When we look at acceptance through the window of T for truth, we realize that we are all an integral part of this Bigger One."

Swamiji looked down for a moment and sipped his tea. A large smile appeared on his face and he let out a chuckle that caught the attention of the room. He realized their surprise by the look on their faces. Clearing his throat, he said, "Please pardon me for my small laugh. I just had a flashback of an incident that occurred during my last visit to the United States. Allow me to share a rather funny story that also reflects what I am trying to explain.

"I was visiting a close friend in New York City by the name of Ash Malhotra. When we were younger, Ash and I spent many days together exploring the uninhabited rugged mountains of the Katmandu area in Nepal. During our adventures," said Swamiji, "we also shared several in-depth, real-life and philosophical discussions. Ash was especially fascinated by the concept of how stress-free motivation could result from aligning ourselves with the Psychology of the Universe.

"Ash founded a very successful computer software business, and his company was always under pressure to develop new products faster than its competitors. He also required ongoing help from his legal firm to protect his intellectual property through copyrights and patents. Needless to say, his staff was very stressed. Ash made me promise that on my next trip here I would speak to his top managers. He wanted me to give them a presentation on the secret of lasting inner motivation that is independent of worldly titles, bonuses and rewards.

"Ash had scheduled a 10 A.M. meeting for me to speak to his management team," said Swamiji. "That morning, he had to drop some files at his attorney's office concerning a new patent application. We were running late and, to save time, Ash took his coffee with him in the car. While he was driving, he tried to take a sip of his coffee, but his hand slipped and the entire cup of hot coffee spilled in his lap.

"I thought he might be upset, but instead he joked with me. 'It's too bad I brought my coffee from home,' he told me. 'There is a distinct advantage in buying your morning coffee from a fast food restaurant—this could have been a million-dollar spill!' We both laughed and I gave him my handkerchief to help him absorb the spilled coffee.

"When we reached the law office I was surprised when Ash told his attorney that he had just been injured by someone's grossly negligent behavior and wanted to bring a lawsuit against this party for that injury. The attorney was also rather surprised, as Ash was always against any legal battles and preferred to settle everything through negotiations.

"Ash's attorney asked him what had happened and why he wanted to pursue this case. Getting impatient, Ash told his attorney to prepare the legal papers and proceed with the claim instead of asking any more questions.

"The attorney finally gave in and began writing down the information. He asked Ash for the name of the party that he wanted to bring this personal injury case against.

"With slight hesitation Ash replied, 'I want to sue my *right hand* for its gross negligence in causing me personal injury. It spilled a hot cup of coffee into my lap and I suffered serious burns.'

"At first the attorney could not believe what Ash was saying. Then he suddenly burst out laughing. But Ash did not laugh. He insisted that he really wanted to sue his right hand.

"'You have to be kidding, you simply cannot be serious,' his attorney told him.

"'I am very serious about this. Please proceed with your full preparation.' Ash responded sternly. In all of their years together, the attorney had never heard Ash speak so harshly.

"'Do you realize what you are saying?' said his attorney. 'You want to sue yourself! The courts will laugh at you and me both, and throw this case out immediately. They may even inflict a fine for wasting the court's time and resources,' his attorney pleaded.

"Ash stood up, looked into his attorney's eyes and said, 'But that is what we do every day. We sue each other thinking that we are separate entities. The fact of the matter is that we are not separate entities, but an inseparable part of the Bigger One.'"

Being an attorney herself, Marcie pounced upon the practicality of the principle at work in Ash's situation. "Swamiji, if I agree with this logic of

Oneness, how do you propose we operate in this society without holding individuals responsible for their actions?"

Swamiji looked at Marcie compassionately. "We must always realize that whatever *one* person does ultimately affects us *all*. Our society has paid a very heavy penalty for taking action based on our misunderstanding that we are individuals, rather than integral parts of the Bigger One."

Swamiji took a deep breath, closed his eyes a moment and said, "We must also further realize that the highest achievements of this human race have only come about when our thoughts and actions completely endorse the Oneness of our society, the real truth."

The room remained silent as Swamiji's words resonated in their minds. Even so, the uncertainty in Marcie's eyes was a sign that she longed for further explanation. With a smile, Swamiji said, "There are two sides of the acceptance thought process. The first is the side of truth. Acceptance cannot happen until we fully comprehend and live the truth — the real truth that we are *one*. The second side of acceptance relates to the design of this human system, our human body. What are we truly designed to do?

"We must always realize
that whatever one
person does ultimately
affects us all."

"To fully understand this second side of acceptance, let's look through the window of truth. Visualize hammering a nail into the wall, but you miss the nail and hit your left thumb. The pain inflicted on the left hand is really only experienced by the body," said Swamiji. "No person is going to punish their right hand, because the right and left hands are attached to the same body. Instead, we learn from the experience and prevent it from happening again, but we would never consider cutting off our hands!"

"But Swamiji," Marcie replied, "if I hit myself with a hammer, it's an accident. What I'm referring to is when people purposely plan and commit horrible murders, destroy property and steal from their neighbors."

"Unfortunately, Marcie, we have also seen many examples where people take their own lives, burn their own homes or even harm their own children," Swamiji replied. "The real question is 'why'? Why do people do these things to strangers, their loved ones, and even to themselves?"

"But most of the time people who harm themselves or their loved ones are emotionally disturbed or mentally sick," Marcie explained. "I'm referring to normal people who commit vicious, premeditated crimes in broad daylight. I feel they should be held responsible for their actions. What's wrong with my thinking?"

Swamiji responded in a very soft voice, "Marcie, just like these people you are calling mentally disturbed or sick, a similar sickness lives in the people who are stealing, lying or cheating others at the moment of their action. But their sickness is in the form of ego, insecurity, fear, greed, anger, hatred and other self-centered factors. Even though we may not call them sicknesses, they truly are contaminants that influence and control our actions."

Swamiji paused for a moment. "We must understand that just as there are a thousand ways for our bodies to be sick, there is only one way to be healthy. Being healthy is the simplest state of our system, free of all sickness and disease.

"Similarly," he said, "there could be a thousand reasons to commit a crime, behave irresponsibly or be contaminated. But there is only one way to be completely free of all these contaminations and operate in complete harmony with how our system was designed. When our human system is free of contamination, it is free of disease. Our complete harmony only comes about when we are void of duality, not thinking as I, Me, My and Mine and living in the absence of segregated thinking."

Susie interjected, "Swamiji, what do you mean

"There are a thousand
ways for our bodies
to be sick,
but there is only one
way to be healthy."

when you keep referring to 'how our system was designed'?"

Swamiji grinned. "Please allow me to ask you a simple question. If you are asked to drive an automobile from one end of your city to the other end in *reverse*, what are your chances of having an accident? Wouldn't it be terribly stressful and frustrating?"

"Not if Ron was driving his Hummer," Susie joked. Laughter filled the room.

Swamiji chuckled and said, "Susie, you have to admit, cars are not designed to be driven long distances in reverse."

"I understand that, Swamiji, but how does that relate to our 'human system'?" asked Susie.

"Just like cars are not designed to be driven in reverse for long distances," Swamiji said, "similarly our human system is not designed to be self-centered. It is only when we act as a separate entity that we operate with a mentality of fear, greed, anger and ego, and we deviate from how our human system was originally designed.

"In the short time that we are on this earth, we are designed for serving and giving to our Bigger One unconditionally," Swamiji continued. "This means we cannot have any self-centered hidden agendas, prejudices, greed, fear or hesitation. When we have a selfish focus, it is equivalent to our driving that car in reverse against its fundamental design."

Ron decided to get involved in the discussion. "This all makes sense, Swamiji," he said. "But Marcie is talking about hardened criminals who hurt our society and this doesn't answer her original question. Don't we need to hold these people responsible for their selfish actions?"

"Ron," Swamiji said, "we need to hold these individuals responsible to the point that they cannot continue to harm our Bigger One, our society. I am talking about a mindset that we must have to prevent further sickness from infecting our society. We must find the reasons why we have so many people who become criminals. The moment we think of others as a separate entity, rather than acknowledging that we are all part of the Bigger One, we unknowingly deviate from how we have been designed. As a result, we become insensitive to the feelings of everyone else around us," he said. "This insensitivity, coupled with a self-centered agenda that goes unfulfilled, often builds into stress and anger. Sometimes these even lead to our own hateful and revengeful criminal activities.

"When we look at our own bodies, this concept

of unconditional serving becomes even more obvious. There are many different parts of the body and each has its own design and purpose; however, there is no body part that can serve itself," he said.

"For example, our hand can perform many functions, but it cannot serve itself. The right hand cannot think or move independently. When it becomes injured, it lies helpless, depending on the body to take care of it. It is only through the strengthening of the body that the hand becomes strong. You see, the hand is only as strong as the body it is attached to. And, it is only when the hand serves its entire body that the hand can ultimately be served by the bigger body."

Engrossed in the conversation, Manny leaned forward and said, "Swamiji, this has far-reaching implications, but I am still not quite clear about this thought process of unconditional acceptance, especially when we are subjected to situations when no one else is practicing acceptance and they throw a monkey wrench into our plans. I don't see how we can practice acceptance when unacceptable things happen."

Swamiji listened with understating to Manny's perspective and said, "Please allow me to share another story with you."

There was a very powerful and demanding king who was known for his very short attention span. He was continuously changing his mind and never content with any situation. He had two extremely well-educated, intelligent and talented assistants by the name of Raj and Ravi, who were always ready to serve him.

Raj had a highly analytical mind and continuously tried to decipher the reasoning behind the king's orders. He would become utterly frustrated when the king's desires and logic did not make any sense to him, and Raj would then unnecessarily debate the king's demands and decisions with Ravi.

Ravi, on the other hand, followed the king's orders with a smile and went about his daily tasks retaining his ultimate faith in the king's wisdom.

One late afternoon the king called Raj and Ravi onto his terrace and instructed them to straighten the garden and turn the soil. He then turned away and left.

Raj started grumbling and said, "I am not trained to do this. There is a gardener that comes every day and the king wants me to work in the garden? I don't have any tools! What am I supposed to do?"

While Raj was complaining, Ravi found the toolbox, gave Raj a small shovel and they both began working. However, only a few minutes passed before the gardener came by and demanded his tools. The king had ordered his gardener to work on the outer garden because he was expecting some important guests.

Raj could not believe that the king had acted this way again. "Look at what he does. He orders me to do something and then takes away my tools. Am I supposed to use my fingers?"

As Raj continued to complain and make excuses, Ravi looked around the garden area and found a long branch. He improvised and made the branch into a tool to turn the soil.

The king was sitting on his terrace and saw Raj moving in circles and talking to himself. The king then went to the garden and asked Raj, "Why are you not working? I told you to turn the soil in the garden."

Raj sheepishly looked at the king and responded, "The gardener took my tools, Sir. I do not have any tools to work with."

The king saw that Ravi was already done with half the garden, while Raj was still in the same spot where he had started. The king grew upset and screamed at his servant. "Why are you always coming up with excuses? I hired you because you are intelligent and talented. Be creative and think! Look at Ravi. He has taken a branch and made it into a tool. You should never be a slave of circumstance, condition or expectations."

David chimed in, excited to share his thoughts. "I get it! We are supposed to be like Ravi and accept what comes, then make the best of the situation, improvise, innovate and remain focused on our overall objective."

Tony nodded in agreement with David's comment and added, "…and not be swayed by outside forces."

"Instead," David continued, "we act like Raj, letting our expectations and emotions to get in the way."

Swamiji smiled at David's enthusiasm. "That is the true power of acceptance, my friends. But it is only available to us when we leave the baggage of the past behind and live in the present without any expectations, self-created boundaries or limitations."

Mona had been quietly absorbing the conversation, but could not refrain from making a comment that was based on her firsthand experience in the United States. She had come to this country from her native home of India just five years earlier.

"Swamiji," Mona said, "since you were educated in America and also have the experience of working here, you will be easily able to relate to what I have to say. Then I hope you may be able to clarify my confusion. The United States is basically a 'take-charge' society where nothing is considered impossible. How can you explain this acceptance paradigm relative to the stunningly successful history of the American opposition to practicing acceptance?"

Pausing only to take a breath, Mona continued. "Furthermore, in my home country of India, everyone

"The true power of acceptance is only available to us when we live without any expectations, self-created boundaries or limitations."

talks about 'accepting God's will.' Millions of people
simply live in the most depressed conditions without
challenging what is imposed upon them; thus, they do
not take charge of their lives. Although your examples
make perfect sense, Swamiji, why do these real-world
examples appear to contradict the thought process of
'acceptance'?"

Everyone wondered what Swamiji was thinking.
Mona had posed a difficult question and they were
curious to hear his reply.

Swamiji smiled. "To answer your question, we
not only have to *make* our special *TEA* using our new
recipe, consisting of T for truth, E for expectations and
A for acceptance, but we also need to *serve* this *TEA*.

"This is a very unique and extremely potent *TEA*,
and it simply cannot be made with *ordinary* water. Nor
can it be held or served in any ordinary cup. To make
this empowering *TEA*, we will need special water and
a unique cup so that we can serve and drink and gain
the full benefits of this most life-changing *TEA*."

There was great surprise as everyone had thought
that the wisdom represented in the letters compris-
ing *TEA* disclosed the *complete* recipe. The assembled
group of friends simply could not wait to unveil the
rest of the puzzle.

"We not only have
to make our special TEA
using our new recipe,
consisting of T for truth,
E for expectations
and A for acceptance,
but we also need
to serve this TEA."

Chapter Five

Making and Serving the TEA

Fresh hot tea was poured and more of Anju's and Patty's homemade treats were passed around. All eyes were fixed on Swamiji with renewed alertness. With an enthusiastic look on his face, Swamiji asked, "Is everyone now ready to learn how to make the TEA?"

Everyone nodded.

"It is essential that we find the right water to make our special TEA," Swamiji said. "In our daily life, we notice that contaminants such as excess chlorine or the pungent-smelling sulfur that is in some well water will significantly affect the taste of the tea. Or if we use water from a lake that has been badly polluted, that tea, even with the highest quality and most valuable ingredients, probably will still make us very sick.

"We have to first realize and always remember that this is not an ordinary tea. This *TEA* can change our lives by bringing us in harmony with our inner selves and with the Universe that surrounds us," he said. "This *TEA* can free us from all the miseries and pains associated with worldly living. Therefore, it is crucial that we fully comprehend the unique characteristics of the very special water required to make our life-changing *TEA*.

"To give you a glimpse of these characteristics and to further help us comprehend the *TEA*, please allow me to share another story with you. Before I begin, however, I feel I must warn you. This is a very painful and real story. Every time I remember and think of this story, it causes enormous agony and brings tears to my eyes. Yet it unveils the essence of what we are talking about, and I need to share it with all of you."

Nima was a young woman who loved children and always wanted to help those with learning disabilities. She had the incredible gift of compassion, coupled with unlimited patience. Her husband, Alex, knew that he could never find a better mother for his children. He always dreamed about having a home full of kids, as he was himself a 'kid' who in many ways had never grown up. It was this childlike freshness in Alex that Nima fell in love with. She knew she was very fortunate to find such a loving and kind husband who would do anything to make her happy.

Alex and Nima wanted to start their family right away, but after two years they had not succeeded in conceiving a child. They approached experts at the local hospitals and went through many series of tests. Eventually, they were referred to a specialist at a world-renowned clinic. More tests were done there, and after three years of thorough evaluations, Alex and Nima finally learned that Nima would not be able to conceive. Alex and Nima were heartbroken.

Alex simply could not bear Nima's pain and suggested that they adopt a child. After all, it was their love that they wanted to share with a child that was the most important thing. Nima agreed and they approached a few adoption agencies to see if they could qualify. To their surprise, one of the agencies called them back right away. They had an unusual situation. A three-year-old boy named Jimmy was immediately available. When they went to see him, there was such an inviting smile in the eyes of this baby that they were compelled to say 'yes' on the spot. All the paperwork was rushed through, and they brought the baby home in a week.

Although they had wanted a child for such a long time, Alex and Nima had no idea that one little baby could bring so much joy to their lives. Every living moment was filled with thoughts of him, and they spent hours with him talking and playing. They simply loved their angel. Almost instantly, Alex and Nima had completely forgotten the pain and memories of their inability to have their own baby.

A few months after they brought Jimmy home, Nima received a call from the head of the last fertility clinic she had visited. With great excitement in his voice, the doctor told Nima that they had had a major breakthrough and would like to see her right away.

There was a good chance that they could now help her conceive!

This news brought tears of joy to Nima's eyes, and the first thing she did was to pick up little Jimmy. She hugged and kissed him as tears rained from her eyes. In her mind, she was sure that this new good fortune was only happening because of the luck that little Jimmy had brought into their lives.

Many little things suddenly fell into place. Alex got a big promotion and became head of his department. Nima was offered a key position in a local institute where she was in charge of designing and implementing an educational program for children. Even the couple's ridiculously low offer to purchase a house they could not afford, but absolutely wanted to have, was accepted.

Most importantly, the clinic's experiment was a success. Alex and Nima were blessed with their own little Jeremy. Now four years old, little Jimmy was the happiest of all. He could not do enough for his little brother, and he was a real help to Nima. Jimmy had

a certain way about him. He felt deep gratitude towards his parents. His ever-present
smile was there even when he was in pain
or hurting. Unlike most children, he never
complained or asked for anything.

Although Nima loved both Jeremy and
Jimmy as only a mother could, she knew
that Jimmy was something special. She
could not believe how such a young person,
not yet even aware of what life was about,
could always exhibit such a totally unselfish
and loving demeanor.

Alex, however, was partial towards
Jeremy, whom he considered to be more of
his own. He fulfilled Jeremy's every demand
and fancy and, as time passed, Alex's leni-
ency and special favoring spoiled him.

Swamiji looked down for a moment, hesitated
briefly and then continued.

Alex would make comments to Nima that
she should pay more attention to their own
son, as he was their flesh and blood. Nima
became very upset with these words, and

they would often have heated arguments.

All of this was getting embedded into Jeremy's subconscious, and he was developing a sort of jealous hatred for his brother. He began to think that Jimmy was stealing his mother's love from him. Jeremy resented any attention Nima gave to his brother, which in his way of thinking was rightfully his own. Jeremy did not understand the concept of being grateful, and he thought it was his right to have everything that he was given. Nothing was ever enough for Jeremy, and he became very upset if he did not get his way.

On the other hand, Jimmy was always grateful for even the smallest things. Rather than complaining or asking, his entire agenda was to give and help others. He was very good in his studies and was eager to help other students in his classes. Jimmy was the favorite of his entire school. He graduated at the top of his class and was awarded a full scholarship to a prestigious college just outside of Washington, DC.

Nima was very proud of Jimmy, but Alex was only relieved that he would not need to fund Jimmy's college education. Jeremy was happy that his brother was away from him so he now could enjoy total freedom and finally master his own destiny.

Jeremy and even Alex did not realize that through the years Jimmy had kept a loving and watchful eye on Jeremy's activities and had many times saved his brother from getting into trouble.

Now, without his older brother's guidance and influence, Jeremy was left with very little supervision. Nima and Alex were at the peak of their careers and had little time to watch him closely. As a result, Jeremy began to associate with the wrong crowd, and learned their bad habits.

Alex always felt that he was not giving Jeremy the attention that he needed, so for his 16th birthday, he bought Jeremy a sports car in spite of Nima's objections. New wheels gave Jeremy even more freedom and a tool to impress his materialistic friends. One night he went to a party and heavily indulged in drugs and alcohol. Some of his friends asked him not to drive in that condition, but no one could ever stop Jeremy from doing what he wanted to do. As he tried to drive home, Jeremy lost complete control of his car and ran into a concrete barrier. This accident not only left him with several broken bones, but it also ruptured both of his kidneys, which could not be saved. He was put on dialysis, and doctors added his name to a long list of patients in need of a kidney transplant.

When Jimmy learned about this tragic accident, he immediately rushed to the hospital. Without informing his parents, he asked to be tested for the compatibility of his kidney. He was thrilled to learn that he was a match, and asked to immediately proceed as an organ donor. Jimmy also asked that his identity as the donor be kept a complete secret from his family, especially from his brother. Nima and Alex were surprised and could not understand why Jimmy was not present to support his brother during the surgery and never even called to check on his progress until days later.

Shifting in his chair and slightly hesitating, Swamiji continued.

The operation was a complete success and Jeremy made a full recovery. However, instead of being grateful that his life had been saved, Jeremy felt cheated. He felt that he was young, and now he could not live a 'free' life, as the doctors had warned him to refrain from drugs, alcohol and bad eating habits. Jeremy was now even more angry with and jealous of his brother, whom he thought still had both of his kidneys and did not even think enough of him to show up for his operation. He wondered why nothing bad ever happened to Jimmy.

Jeremy never faced the facts that he had chosen to indulge in drugs and excessive drinking and that he had ignored his friends when they asked him not to drive in that condition. Despite the tragedy that he experienced because of his poor choices and negligence, he showed no gratitude that an anonymous donor had saved his life. He ignored his great fortune that many people must wait for years to find their matching donors, and many never do.

Jeremy had been given a new lease on life, allowing him to pursue all of its opportunities. But he chose not to be grateful for this great gift. As time passed, the hatred and jealousy that burned within Jeremy completely poisoned him and caused him to experience a deep state of depression. Jimmy tried to cheer him up, but that made Jeremy even worse because he simply could not stand to see his brother's smiling face. He thought Jimmy was only smiling because he still had both of his kidneys and everyone would see him as the 'better brother.' Jeremy never accepted the conditions that he was placed in and blamed everyone else.

Swamiji's tone became more somber as he gazed at the intent faces of the group.

This depressed state of Jeremy's mind

adversely affected his overall health, and he was readmitted into the hospital.

It so happened that one of the doctors who had assisted in his transplant was making his rounds in the same ward where Jeremy was admitted. This doctor spoke with him, and after discussing his medical condition, he asked about his brother's health. Jeremy was greatly surprised that the doctor even knew he had a brother, and even more surprised that he asked about his health. He had never known Jimmy to be sick.

The doctor was not aware of Jimmy's strict request to keep his kidney donation confidential. Innocently, he blurted out that he had never witnessed such an act of unconditional love as Jimmy's eager willingness to give his own kidney to save his brother's life. Jeremy was sure that the doctor was mistaken and told him that no one knew who had donated the kidney.

The doctor was taken aback that Jeremy did not know the facts. He looked directly into his eyes and told him, "My friend, it was my hands that removed your brother's kidney. It is his kidney that has given you a new lease on life. I am surprised that your family never told you this."

As the doctor was saying his last few words, Alex and Nima entered the hospital room. Nima asked, "What did we not tell him, doctor?"

The doctor looked at Alex and Nima and said, "I informed your son that the kidney keeping him alive was donated by his brother. Is there a reason that Jeremy was never told? You knew this, didn't you?"

"No, we did not know," Alex replied. "We were only told by the hospital that Jeremy was very fortunate that they found a matching kidney for him. Are you sure that you are not mistaken, or maybe confusing Jeremy with someone else?"

Alex was skeptical of this surprising news, but Nima immediately knew that this was the truth. No one else would make this noble sacrifice in total anonymity other than her angel, Jimmy.

Jeremy thought about all that had happened and soon realized that it was the truth. But for him, this one answer created more questions.

What really confused him was how his brother could still be so happy and smiling, even after losing one of his kidneys. If he had been needed to donate his kidney to Jimmy, he was not sure he could have done it. And if he had been able to, he surely could not ever see himself being happy about living the rest of his life with the risk of having only one kidney.

Jeremy's thoughts were interrupted by his mother hugging him. With tears streaming down her cheeks, Nima told him, "Jeremy, you are so fortunate to have a brother who loves you so much that he would risk his life for you without even letting any of us know about his sacrifice."

At this moment Swamiji paused and sighed, hesitating even to start speaking again. "It is very painful for me to share the rest of this story with you, but I must," and he took a deep breath.

In his depressed and totally self-centered state of mind, Jeremy suddenly felt that he knew the answer to his question. He was sure that his brother gave him his kidney so that Jimmy could forever establish his superiority in the eyes of their mother.

Even worse, Jeremy could not believe that his mother was not able to see his brother's evil and manipulative act. If Jimmy had really wanted to help, why did he not just find someone else to give him a kidney?

Swamiji looked down and put his hands in his lap. He began speaking again slowly. His heart ached to continue with the story.

Jeremy thought that he could never forgive his brother for his act of deceit and phoniness. He become furious and started shouting, "I do not want Jimmy's kidney inside of me. Please doctor, take it out. I hate him. He always wins and gets his way. I hate him, I hate him. I wish I never had a brother." Jeremy became so violent that the doctors had to give him a sedative to calm him down.

With his eyes closed, Swamiji could feel the pain this story had brought into the hearts of his audience. The room was silent.

Ron had been listening intently to Swamiji's story, but thought he was now getting conflicting messages. He said, "Swamiji, that is a very sad yet powerful story. But I do not understand how it relates to the wisdom of the letters T-E-A."

Tony suddenly came alive in the conversation and said, "On the contrary, Ron, this story brings everything Swamiji has been saying into a very clear focus, at least for me. For example, Jimmy was living the T for truth, as he was practicing the concept of Oneness. In spite of Jeremy's obvious hatred towards him, Jimmy saw no difference between himself and his brother and gave up his kidney without any judgment, hesitation or hidden motives."

"And conversely," David observed, "in the absence of truth, Jeremy's entire life of suffering and pain came from *not* practicing this Oneness."

"And the E was also in the story," noted Marcie. "Jeremy always had expectations, and they were always unrealistic and self-centered. There was no way that he could ever be satisfied. It is easy to see how he ended up in total depression."

"Jeremy also never understood the wisdom of A for acceptance," Mona shared. "Although he had been given a new lease on life, he only longed for what was in the past, rather than accepting and living in the present."

"What got to me was Jeremy's complete absence of gratefulness for his brother," Anju said with disappointment in her voice. "You would really think he would have felt thankful when he learned that Jimmy had risked his own life to save his, especially without wanting any acknowledgment."

Swamiji remained silent as he watched how everyone participated in the conversation, each sharing their understanding of the afternoon's dialogue. Then Susie asked him, "Swamiji, what about the special water you said we need to make our TEA?"

Swamiji replied, "Our *TEA* must be prepared using uncontaminated water that consists of complete gratefulness. When we fully understand and humbly live the truth, this places us in the unconditional mode of gratefulness. And the proper mindset of expectation and acceptance cannot be practiced without gratefulness. Simply stated, our recipe of *TEA* must be prepared in the water of *gratefulness* in every living moment."

Anju was puzzled at these words and asked, "I can see how gratefulness must have a foundation of acceptance and expectation, but I do not understand the connection between truth and gratefulness, Swamiji. Could you please explain that again?"

Swamiji smiled lovingly at Anju. "Recall when we discussed the story of the Prince and Murli. And how we must understand and practice the real truth, which is the universal thread connecting all individuals to the Bigger One. Our system is designed to operate free of stress only in a mindset of Oneness, which diminishes the selfish importance of I, Me, My and Mine," he said.

"In this pure state, we develop an unwavering and unconditional respect for the Universal Wisdom of this Bigger One, as well as for this same perfect component within everyone we encounter.

"This unconditional respect becomes the foundation for our *gratefulness* that is totally responsible for our abilities, our resources and our very existence from birth to death. And this unconditional respect energizes and sustains us, even as we are surrounded by worldly contaminants."

"Our human system
is designed to operate
in a mindset of Oneness,
which diminishes
the selfish importance
of I, Me, My and Mine."

Swamiji took a deep breath and closed his eyes for a moment. Then he looked up and continued. "Have you ever seen a pond that has become overridden with the growth of trees and other vegetation? The thick algae that covers it prevents us from seeing what lives in the water. Imagine that, suddenly, in the midst of all this chaos and ugliness, there grows a beautiful white lotus flower...flawless, untouched and uncontaminated.

"Our unconditional respect towards the omnipresent Universal Wisdom will produce this perfect lotus of gratefulness within each of us. We will be inspired with enthusiasm and creativity, despite whatever contaminants we encounter in our lives."

Manny was nodding his head and eager to share his newfound understanding of acceptance in the new light of gratefulness. "Now I understand, Swamiji. We must first comprehend truth before we can truly be grateful. And it is only with this grateful mindset that we can practice unconditional acceptance."

Swamiji nodded and added, "In the absence of gratefulness, our *TEA* will always be contaminated by an element of resentment. But the paradigm of acceptance can be a tool of personal empowerment. It redirects our focus from self-pity to knowing our real purpose of life, which is to make a meaningful contribution to our Bigger One, one person and one task at a time."

Swamiji paused for a moment. "But, my friends, we must never impose this thought process of acceptance upon others. Instead, we must always look upon and serve others with total compassion. Being compassionate keeps us within the design of our human system—which is a path of unconditional loving, serving and giving—and allows us to avoid unwanted frustrations and stress."

"Oh, now I understand, Swamiji," said Patty, who had been absorbing every word. "I bet you want us to serve this *TEA* in a cup of *compassion*. Am I right?"

"You are *absolutely* right, Patty." Swamiji answered with great excitement, seeing that his message was being understood. "Our cup of *compassion* must become our perpetual mindset. This mindset of compassion makes us sensitive and motivates us to not accept pain, poverty and injustice for others."

"But most of the time, we do the opposite," Mona said. "We preach to others to accept what life gives them, but we do not practice acceptance in our own lives. We think we deserve better, and we ask why these things happen to us. We always justify every position we take, and we always find someone or something to blame."

"Being compassionate
keeps us within the design
of our human system...
and allows us to avoid
unwanted frustrations
and stress."

"And when we have no choice in the end but to accept, we do so with resentment and never with gratefulness," Patty added.

"We show compassion towards ourselves, but when we see others in pain we simply shrug our shoulders and *walk away*," Anju remarked.

Ron straightened in his chair and said, "Or if we are truly moved by someone in severe pain, we only provide a quick fix instead of a permanent solution."

Tony joined in. "Often, we do not show *true* compassion. We only pretend to care because we think someone is watching or we may get recognition for it."

"Showing compassion towards others must become our basic operating software," Swamiji explained. "It acts as a catalyst, driving us to make a difference in the lives of others. With compassion in our hearts, we simply cannot tolerate seeing someone in pain. Compassion will motivate us to adopt a 'can do' attitude, which Mona noticed originally made America great. Our 'can do' attitude will allow us to overcome the injustice incurred by others. And we will be filled with the creativity and abundant resources of the Universe."

Tony was absorbing every single word. Yet he wondered why everyone doesn't practice compassion. He asked, "Swamiji, is compassion a learned art or do we all have compassion within us? Do we need some sort of training?"

Swamiji shook his head. "That is a very good question Tony, but its answer invokes very deep reflection into what makes each of us *human*. Someone once said, 'The key difference between an animal and a human being is that only a human is capable of showing compassion to a total stranger.' The unfortunate part, Tony, is that so many of us do not rise to the level of our true human potential."

Intrigued by this response, Ron asked, "Is there a way that we can graduate to that 'true human level'?"

Without hesitation, Swamiji responded, "There is a basic habit that one must cultivate to become truly human. I call this our 'founding habit' that will lead to all other habits. Compassion will be a result of—and a by-product of—practicing these combined habits."

Everyone was drawn onto this new wave of Swamiji's ocean of wisdom. They began to wonder what Swamiji was alluding to.

Manny was about to guess what it could be, but hesitated. Sensing his uncertainty, Swamiji asked, "Do you know what the one fundamental habit is, Manny?"

"If my mother were asked this question, she would

say that the basic habit that each of us needs to have is that of 'unconditional loving.'"

In a second breath, Manny continued. "But I never could understand the thought process of loving unconditionally. I mean, there has to be some quality or purpose in loving someone. How could we love someone without any reason?"

Swamiji responded, "I greatly admire the clarity of divine wisdom in your mother, Manny. It is *most definitely* unconditional love that we look for as this founding habit. It is what separates us, and what can change us, from an animal to a true human."

Swamiji paused briefly and continued, "Manny, your question and argument are valid. We often feel that we need a reason to love someone. But what if I told you that there is something special, unique and absolutely flawless that is already present in every person? Would you be able to guess what that is?"

David suddenly stood up. "Oh, my God, Swamiji, I cannot believe it. You are talking about the presence of Divinity in all of us, aren't you? This is the only thing that can be flawless and lovable without any reservations or conditions. It is the Divinity in all of us that actually unites us to the 'Bigger One' you've been talking about."

David continued, "And, if we have unconditional love for the Divinity within each of us, we will be utterly grateful and have compassion towards everyone."

Swamiji got up and hugged David. Tears filled Swamiji's eyes.

Anju was deeply touched to see the genuine love and respect between the two men she loved so dearly. As she looked around the room, she realized in her mind that the ten bodies that had joined together for this discussion had now been transformed into a single soul. She wished that this very special moment could last forever, but she also knew the time was coming for Swamiji to depart.

"My dear friends," Swamiji said, "the time has come to say good-bye. I shall always treasure this afternoon."

"Oh please, Swamiji, you cannot go yet," said Anju. "We have only just begun. There are so many more mysteries that you can help us understand!"

Swamiji looked deeply into Anju's eyes and replied, "There is something that we all must make peace with during our rather short stay on this earth. It doesn't matter how many educational degrees we earn, or how extensive our worldly experiences are, or how much we share in wonderful discussions like this one." He took a long breath and said, "Ultimately, the Universe will still remain a mystery to us all."

Everyone thought about these words in silence, and then Patty spoke. "Swamiji, I have spent my whole life trying to help people understand why and how people do what they do. You are truly one of the most enlightened teachers I have ever met. Are you really saying that this is all still a mystery to *you*?"

Swamiji replied, "Patty and my dear friends, it takes an incredible amount of knowledge, experience, intelligence and education just for us to realize how much we do not know. We are just not *designed* to find the ultimate answer, and all things are simply not within our reach and human capacity.

"There was once a brilliant Nobel Prize-winning space scientist who was asked by a journalist, 'How close are we to finding the ultimate answer to the Universe's mysteries?' The scientist replied, 'We are not any closer. The problem is that each new discovery we make results in a million more that become visible for us to explore and unveil. Anytime we learn or answer one thing, there are a million more questions that appear in front of us.'"

Swamiji looked into the eyes of his attentive audience. "Our bodies, our brains and our human system are not designed to comprehend the mysteries of the Universe. That is why people who have an agenda of finding answers in order to take control of what's around them only become stressed and frustrated in the end.

"Our human system is only designed to love, serve and give to the Bigger One. Any new inventions and discoveries we make should be to elevate our capabilities to do these things," he said.

"The most amazing part of this entire journey is that it will give us our true inner happiness, our ultimate security and our real success that is totally independent of all outside factors. And the greatest part is that all of this can be absolutely within our reach, simply by drinking this special *cup of TEA*.

"T is for truth, always keeping the truth in front of us. The truth is that we are not alone. I am not a separate entity. I am not this human body. The truth is that what resides within me is Universal Energy and Wisdom — and it is this same Universal Power that resides in everyone else. This knowledge transforms me into a totally and perpetually grateful entity.

"Our human system
is not designed
to comprehend
the mystery
of the Universe.
That is why people
who have an agenda
of finding answers
in order to take control
of what's around them
only become stressed
and frustrated
in the end."

"As a result, I begin to live in the present rather than becoming lost in my E, which stands for expectations. Expectations waste my time dwelling in a past filled with glories or miseries, or in a future filled with speculations and fears.

"The thought process of gratefulness prepares me for A, the acceptance of whatever comes to me with the grace of complete gratefulness. Thus, I become a 'take-charge' person rather than a victim, making things happen instead of letting them happen.

"If we look at a piece of iron," Swamiji continued, "it has the potential to become an extremely powerful magnet. But it only becomes a magnet when its inner structure gets realigned through an electromagnetic force. While every piece of iron has this potential, very few ever become this powerful.

"My friends, just as every bar of steel has this potential, so does every person who has ever walked this earth. The wisdom hidden within *TEA* can align our human system, empower us beyond anything we could ever have imagined and ultimately set us free from stress and frustration."

Taking one last sip of his tea, Swamiji turned to survey the faces that circled the room. "Always remember this recipe for TEA, and it will make an incredible difference in your lives." With these words, Swamiji joined his hands together and bowed to his audience as a sign of respect and gratefulness.

Patty stepped forward. Without saying a word, she respectfully placed the palms of her hands together and bowed to Swamiji. Swamiji smiled and opened his arms to Patty. She wrapped him in a light loving embrace. Her voice cracked with emotion as she said, "Thank you, Swamiji. Thank you for opening my heart and mind to life's mysteries."

Others in the room wished to express their own heartfelt emotions to Swamiji. Several members of the group made their farewells with graceful bows and words of affection. Some were moved to wordless tears of gratitude.

Their frustration and stress had now completely disappeared and they now knew the recipe for stress-free living.

All were clearly awash in feelings of loving gratefulness and the enlightenment that they had shared in their short time together.

Each and all understood that on that day their vision of their place in the universe had changed.

Swamiji's Prayer

"Lord, I do not know
what I want. I do not know
what is good for me.
Please help me experience
the joy of life
by giving me wisdom
and the resources
to add the highest value."

About the Author

A successful entrepreneur, polymer technologist, educator, author, lecturer, television and radio personality and family man, Ratanjit S. Sondhe has traveled around the world speaking to students, homemakers and professionals, young and old, delivering such life-changing messages as "Determine Your Passion," "Overcoming Life's Obstacles," "Finding Peace in the Midst of Chaos," "Leadership from Within" and many others.

Ratanjit has authored several books and papers including his internationally award-winning work, "Philosophy of Quality." His 10-year radio program and international television show has touched the lives of many with simple expressions of wisdom that empower individuals to find personal success, joy and internal peace.

Ratanjit also dedicates his time serving on the board of many community, service and non-profit organizations.

More information is available online at www.ratanjit.com.

Also Written by the Author

The Secret of our Ultimate Success

102 Quotes to Realign our Life

Also Available from the Author
Ratanjit's Visions Radio Series

- "Finding Peace in the Midst of Chaos"
- "Overcoming Mediocrity"
- "The Secret of Making a Marriage Last"
- "Searching for Faith, Hope and Love"
- "Coping with Personal Tragedy"
- "Leadership from Within"
- "Building Wealth through Spirituality"
- "The Master Key"
- And hundreds more

Visit www.ratanjit.com for a complete listing
of books, CDs and downloadable audio programs.

TEA: The Recipe for Stress-Free Living

is also available:

E-Book

Audio Book

Internet downloadable audio file

TEA Book Gift Set

TEA Companion Book: Drinking the TEA

TEA: Group Discussion Guide & Workbook

Special Online Editions are also available.

Visit www.ratanjit.com for
a complete catalogue listing.

You're Invited to Join Swamiji's TEA Club

Continue the journey and join the discussion of TEA with Swamiji and friends at www.teaclub.org.

Ratanjit and discoverhelp publishing kindly extend an invitation to you for a complimentary one-year membership to Swamiji's TEA Club.

Ask questions about the book, learn more about the characters, have online chat sessions with the author and more. Swamiji's TEA Club is a safe haven for individuals of like-minded thoughts to discuss the frustrations of daily living and realign habits to achieve success on the path of Truth.

Along with your membership, you also receive special discounts and access to member-only online editions of the TEA Companion Book and Group Discussion Guide & Workbook.